A Woman
After
God's Own
Heart®

A DEVOTIONAL

ELIZABETH GEORGE

HARVEST HOUSE PUBLISHERS
EUGENE, OREGON

Cover by Aesthetic Soup, Nashville, Tennessee

A WOMAN AFTER GOD'S OWN HEART®—A DEVOTIONAL
Copyright © 2007 Elizabeth George
Published by Harvest House Publishers
Eugene, Oregon 97402
www.harvesthousepublishers.com

ISBN 978-0-7369-5966-7 (hardcover)
ISBN 978-0-7369-5968-1 (eBook)

Printed in China

20 21 22 23 / RDS-JH / 10 9 8 7 6 5 4 3

A Note from Elizabeth

Imagine living in such a way that people think of you as a woman after God's heart. Better yet, imagine placing God foremost in your heart each morning and striking out on His path for your day, deliberately living for Him. As you commit yourself to God each day, He will work in your heart!

I pray these devotions for busy women like you will help inspire you to draw nearer to God and live out His plans for you. How is this done? The answer: via small steps with big results—living God's way… one day at a time, practicing God's order of priorities for you…one day at a time, committing the many different areas of your life to God…one day at a time.

Treat yourself to jewels of wisdom based on God's Word each day. Enjoy the scriptures and messages in this devotional created just for you, a woman who loves the Lord with all her heart. Be inspired to grow. Be willing to change. Be encouraged to take bold steps in handling your problems or facing difficulties. Most of all, become more knowledgeable of God's character and His great love for you.

May your journey to greater faith and trust in God be filled with joy and delight!

Elizabeth George

I Give Myself to You

We all make choices in what we do with our day. A favorite verse of mine ends with the words, "Charm is deceitful and beauty is vain, but a woman who fears the LORD, she shall be praised" (Proverbs 31:30 NASB). I don't want to be robbed of even one of God's riches by not taking time to let Him invade my life. The bottom line? I want to be a woman after God's own heart!

Make a daily commitment to God. It can be as simple as praying, "Lord, today I give myself anew to You!" Your heart for God should be like a boiling pot—intense and passionate. There's no way to ignore that kind of fire! Be excited to meet God.

Lord, I commit my life to You. Help me be a witness to Your gracious power and love. Amen.

Stop Complaining

I want to say this as nicely as possible: It's time to stop complaining. In Philippians 4:11-13 the apostle Paul writes, "I have learned to be content whatever the circumstances. I know what it is to be in need, and I know what it is to have plenty. I have learned the secret of being content in any and every situation, whether well fed or hungry, whether living in plenty or in want. I can do all this through him who gives me strength" (NIV).

Never once do we see Paul quitting, having a fit, or complaining. Regardless of his predicament, he was content. Why? Because he looked to his Savior for strength. The Bible says to be steadfast, always abounding in the work of the Lord. And when you do, you're on the way to becoming the best possible woman you can be—a woman who serves the Lord.

Lord, help me look to You for my purpose and my strength. Lead me every day so I can do Your will and serve You to the best of my ability. Amen.

Less and Less Time

Another birthday has come…and gone. I'm painfully aware that there's less and less time for becoming the kind of woman I want to be. But it's also comforting to know that God knows the desires of my heart. In fact, Psalm 37:4 says He's put them there. He knows the daydreaming—and praying—I do about serving Him. And He knows your heart too. Whether you're pushing a stroller, a grocery cart, or an aluminum walker—your life counts. It counts mightily as you face life's challenges with a heart full of devotion to God. Keep choosing to love God, and follow after Him with a whole heart each day.

Lord, in You is my hope, in You is my desire, in You is my strength. I love You. Make my life count in someone's life today. Help me reach out with Your love. Amen.

He Will Direct Your Path

Proverbs 3:6 says, "In all your ways acknowledge Him, and He shall direct your paths." But what does that look like in your daily life? The phone rings and it's bad news or a decision needs to be made. This is where you stop and pray, "God, what do You want me to do here?" Or you're going merrily through your day—and someone says something that really hurts. Before you blurt out a smart retort, sit mentally in God's presence. Ask, "Okay, God, what do You want me to say?" When you do your part, God takes over and does His part: He directs your path...and your mouth! Isn't that great?

Heavenly Father, thank You for meeting me where I am. You care about the big things in my life and You care about the little things. You are amazing! Amen.

Accepting Christ

I pray you've given your heart to the Lord. That you've entered into an eternal relationship with God through His Son, Jesus Christ. My dear sister, if you're unsure about where you stand with God, invite Jesus to be your Savior. When you do, you're welcoming Christ into your life. You become a "new creature" (2 Corinthians 5:17 NASB). All it takes is acknowledging your sin before God. Your prayer might be: "God I want to be Your child, a true woman after Your heart. I acknowledge my sin and receive Your Son, Jesus Christ, into my needy heart, giving thanks that He died on the cross for my sins."

Lord, thank You for hearing my prayer. Thank You for coming to earth so I can be in communion with You. I love You. Amen.

Roots Run Deep

When my mother-in-law was seriously ill, my husband—her only son—was out of the country and unreachable. As I cared for her by the hour, I have to tell you—I was reaching deep into my reservoir! There just wasn't time for my usual quiet times with God. What I found was strength in the many scriptures I'd memorized over the years. I gained energy from the psalms I'd read and from past times I spent alone with God. Those were roots deep into God's truth. And I needed every one of them.

If you're going to be a woman after God's own heart, the support you get from a healthy root system is vital for standing strong in the Lord. Meet with God regularly. Talk to Him through prayer and commune with Him through meditation. Read His wisdom found in His Word.

Heavenly Father, thank You for loving me and caring about me daily. I love that I can come to You in times of stress and weakness, and You will give me strength. Amen.

Something Is Better Than Nothing

If someone asked you to describe your quiet time with God today, what would you say? We know how to pull off parties, weddings, and retreats. And our quiet times should be no different—especially considering the value. What's ideal for you? What would make them quality times? What energizes and refreshes you? Keep in mind that something is always better than nothing. Pick a time that matches your lifestyle—even if it's the middle of the night...or at a lunch break... or in the car. Take out your calendar and make an appointment each day.

Meeting with God is such a vital part of becoming all He created you to be!

Father, it's so hard sometimes to set aside time to meet with You. Life is so demanding—family, friends, work, meetings all pull at me. Time seems so short. Please help me keep my priorities in order so I meet with You every day. Thank You. Amen.

Dream Big

Hmm…1 year…12 months…365 days. That's 8,760 hours! You've got time. So dream big. Dream of being a woman who serves and honors God. Will you do this?

First, describe the woman you want to be—spiritually, that is—in one year. In one year you can attack a weak area in your Christian life and gain victory. You can read through the Bible. You can be mentored by an older woman…or be a mentor to a younger woman in the faith. You can complete training in evangelism or finish a one-year Bible study. You can memorize Scripture. Dawson Trotman was a great Christian statesman. He memorized one verse a day for the first three years of his Christian life—that's a thousand verses! Dream on—and do it!

Lord, I hesitate to dream because I'm afraid of commitment and failure. What if I start out and then get tired or forget? But, Lord, I want to grow in You. I want to become the person You want me to be. Give me a dream…and the strength and passion to carry it out. Amen.

The Woman of Your Dreams

God will take you as far as you want to go—as fast as you want to go. To be that woman of your dreams, that woman after God's own heart, is up to you. Proverbs 4:23 says, "Keep your heart with all diligence, for out of it spring the issues of life." You decide what you will or will not do—whether you'll grow or not. And you also decide the rate at which you'll grow. Will it be hit and miss? Or what I call the measles rate: a sudden rash here and there? Do you believe you can be a woman of God? With God's grace and in His strength you can.

Lord, I want to be Your woman...a woman who loves and serves You. Give me the wisdom and perseverance to grow in my relationship with You. Thank You for giving me this opportunity. Amen.

A Prayer Makeover

I remember the day as if it were yesterday. It was my tenth spiritual birthday. I'd dropped my children off at school and was at my desk—resting before God and rejoicing for being His child. I thought back over the years and, with tears of gratitude, prayed, "Lord, what do You see missing in my spiritual life?" The immediate response was all too clear: "Your prayer life!" That day I wrote in my journal, "I dedicate and purpose to spend the next ten years developing a meaningful prayer life." What a rewarding time it has been putting into motion a complete prayer makeover. And in the process becoming a woman who heartily loves and serves God.

Father, thank You for hearing my prayers. It's so exciting to reach up to You on my own...to not have to go through anybody or anything to talk and listen to You. Amen.

You Didn't Need It

When my husband, Jim, was in seminary, we lived in a tiny house with peeling paint and a living room ceiling about to cave in. All our income went for tuition, rent, and groceries. I desperately needed victory in the area of my heart's desires and dreams. Over and over again I placed everything in God's hands. And a prayer principle was born: "If God doesn't meet it, you didn't need it."

Through the years God has faithfully met the many needs of our family. We've experienced the reality of God's promise that "no good thing will He withhold from those who walk uprightly" (Psalm 84:11). And it's true for you too!

> *Lord, thank You for watching over me and providing for me and those I love. I appreciate all You've done for me, all that You are doing for me, and all that You will do for me. I love You! Amen.*

A Heart that Obeys

I'll never forget the time my daughter wanted to impress her boyfriend—and us—by making brownies. Expecting something wonderful, we had to keep from making faces as we bit into the much-awaited brownies. They were horrible! What happened? When we asked whether she'd done anything special or unique in the baking process, my daughter volunteered, "Oh, I left out the salt. Salt's not good for you."

Because of one missing ingredient the whole batch had to be tossed out. Just as that batch of brownies required several ingredients to become what it was intended to be—there's an ingredient key to us becoming women who follow God's heart. The heart God delights in is one that is compliant, cooperative, and responsive to Him—a heart that obeys!

Lord, so many times I want to do what I want to do...so I don't consult You or think about what I know to be true according to Your Word. Please help me remember that serving and loving You are my top priorities. Amen.

Stop Doing Wrong

Are you doing something that is wrong? Today I'm urging you to stop. I can't make it any simpler than that. The split second you think or do anything that will displease God's heart, stop immediately! This action will train your heart to be responsive to God in all situations. If you gossip—stop. If you think unworthy thoughts—stop. If you have a spark of anger—stop before you act on it. Everyone has experiences like these. They happen to all of us often. But how you respond reveals what's at the core of your heart. Call on the Lord. First John 1:9 promises God is "faithful and just to forgive us our sins and to cleanse us from all unrighteousness."

Father God, You are amazing! Not only are You faithful and just to forgive me my sins, but You also cover me with Your grace when I fail to live up to Your standards. Thank You for Your mercy. Amen.

A Servant Woman

First Peter 4:10 says, "Each of you should use whatever gift you have received to serve others, as faithful stewards of God's grace in its various forms." If you're not married, this means you serve God, your family and friends, the company you work for, and people at church and in the community. If you're married, this servant attitude starts with your husband.

It took a few years, but I finally figured out that I'm on assignment from God to help my husband, Jim. I can honestly say I became a better wife—and a better Christian—when I became a better helper. According to God's plan, I'm not to compete with, but to be solidly behind my husband. I'm to be supportive. How does this translate into daily life? Jim is the one I'm supposed to help first, to assist in making his every victory possible.

Lord, I'm so selfish most of the time. Help me combat this tendency and look to You for the strength and wisdom to set my own wants and desires aside and serve the people You've asked me to serve. Amen.

Submission?

"It's time I did something for me for a change!" Sue wanted to quit her job for full-time ministry, and she came to me for counsel. When I asked what her husband had to say, she said, "Oh, he's not a Christian. He doesn't want me to do it." Others told Sue to go ahead and pursue her dream, but the Bible is clear in its instructions. Wives are to "submit" to their own husbands (Ephesians 5:22).

As long as your husband isn't asking you to violate God's Word, as a woman who serves Him, you are to submit. It's by faith in a sovereign God that you and I trust Him to work in our lives directly through our husbands. It may not be popular today, but it's a truth found in the Bible.

Jesus, create in my heart the desire to serve my husband...and the other people You've placed in my life. Give me the strength, patience, and gentleness I need to fully model Your love to them. Amen.

Make Your Husband #1

Talk to your mother about recipes, skills, interests, the Bible, and spiritual growth—but not about your husband. If you haven't already, decide right now to make your husband your Number One human relationship. And that includes making him a priority over your children. Counselors will tell you that the point where marriages most often jump the track is in overinvesting in children and underinvesting in the marriage. Ask yourself, "Am I spoiling my husband rotten?" There's nothing wrong with doing everything in your power to please your husband. That's what loving him is all about. Invest your time, your heart, and your life in prayer for your husband. It's impossible to hate or neglect a person you're praying for!

Lord, help me look at my husband with fresh, loving eyes. I want to see anew all his good qualities...all the things that drew me to him. Give me opportunities to remind him that I love him and why. Amen.

Plan Romance

"Dinner for two? I don't think he's been home in time for dinner in the last month!" Nothing just happens...including a great marriage. Proverbs 21:5 says, "Good planning and hard work lead to prosperity" (NLT). And never is that more true than in a marriage. Plan what I like to call "special deeds of kindness." Run an errand for your husband. Cheer him up. Plan special dinners—dinners he likes. And create special times alone so you can talk and enjoy one another's company. If you're starting to avoid those cozy times—make plans right now to remedy the situation. Loving your husband is part of becoming a woman after God's own heart. Go ahead—lavish love on that husband of yours!

Lord, spark my creativity and help me show my husband how much I love him. Guide me as I make him a priority and encourage him to put time with me on his schedule. Amen.

Developing a Passion for God

I'm sure you have a deep and abiding passion for God's Word. And if you're a mom, you want your kids to know and love God. The Bible says, "Faith comes by hearing, and hearing by the word of God" (Romans 10:17). God's Word provides the knowledge and wisdom your children need to accept Jesus. And if you develop in them a habit of reading the Bible, it will guide them their whole lives! So, as a mother, place God's Holy Scripture first on the list of things your children need to know. And first in your own heart as well. Your passion for Scripture will spill over as you teach your children about Jesus.

Lord, thank You for the incredible blessing of children. I give my precious ones to You. Open their hearts to You and to Your Word. Help me present Your love and guidance in a way that will make them yearn to know You. Amen.

Family First

"Hurry up, girls. We're late as it is!"

I was on a mission of mercy and hurrying my two girls to the car. We were delivering a meal for a friend who'd just had a baby. I'd spent most of the morning preparing a special basket of delicious food. As we started out the door, one of my daughters wanted to know what we were doing and why. I was feeling quite happy with myself as I shared our goal until Katherine asked, "What are *we* having for dinner?"

As I thought about my plan to throw together something quick and easy for my own family, I realized that my priorities weren't exactly in the right order. I was making a special effort to create a delicious meal for someone else…and my own family was getting the short shrift. Ouch!

Lord, You come first in my life…and then comes my family. Help me live those priorities in everything I do—including fixing meals. Amen.

Teach Your Children

What are you teaching your children by the things you say? By what you do? By the places you go? As a mother who knows God, you have the privilege of raising your children to love and follow God. And for that to happen, you have to talk about God to your children—and then back your teachings up with your actions. After all, we talk about and do what's important to us. And when we talk about and follow God's rules, we communicate that He's supremely important to us. Even though children have "selective hearing" at times, the message gets through! So how's your talk? How's your walk?

Lord, it's easy to get caught up in daily duties and forget my children are watching how I think, act, and handle emotions. Help me model Your love, Your values, and Your principles so my children will grow to be loving and responsible. Amen.

The Power of Prayer

"Mom, thanks for praying for me today. It really made a difference!" How blessed we are as mothers to pray for our dear children. And what a delight to set the tone in your home—one of love and laughter, fun and prayer. God makes your heart joyful, generous, giving, happy, and quiet. He enables you to focus on and live out your priorities. And He provides what you need to go the extra mile as a wife and mom. It's not an easy job assignment, but Philippians 4:13 promises that you can do all things through Christ who strengthens you. So lift your heart and your voice to God today. Praise Him for His faithfulness. Thank Him for loving you and for loving your family.

Lord, You are so wonderful. You give me what I need…and then You fulfill the desires of my heart. Thank You for my husband and for my children. You are amazing! Amen.

A Place of Refuge

"If I can just get home, everything will be okay!" Wouldn't it be great if every member of your family knew there was one place where everything will be all right? Your home should be a place of refuge. A place for healing. A place for renewal. Look around your house or apartment…inside and out. Make a list of the things that need to be added, repaired, or set up to create an ambiance of a peaceful haven.

And don't forget your attitude. That's where we're sometimes put to the test. What is that one attitude that if it were improved—transformed by God— would enhance the feel of your home?

I encourage you to take a new look at your home and how people interact there. Take whatever steps you need to improve the sometimes calm, sometimes fun, and always supportive atmosphere at home.

Jesus, I so appreciate having a place my family and I can call home. Bless everyone who walks in our doors. I want my home to echo Your love and care. Amen.

Time Robbers

Do you want to use your time effectively and honor God? Then guard your time carefully. What "time robbers" are in your life? The first one is a ringing phone. You don't always have to answer it! Let the answering machine pick it up. Another problem is being interrupted. Tell people you'll get back to them…and set up a time that's convenient. Failing to delegate also wastes time. And unclear priorities mean you'll probably go on fruitless tangents.

Which of these robbers will you tackle this week so you'll be more efficient and effective as a believer, a woman, a wife, a mother, and a professional?

Oh, and one more thing: Your children are not interruptions. They are your greatest work and the best investment of your time.

Father, I complain I don't have enough hours in my day. I don't get my chores done, I get behind at work, I skip my Bible study, I throw something together for dinner. With Your help I want to be more focused, more efficient, more consistent. Amen.

Diet and Exercise

Every time I ask a woman who's enjoying an energetic life and ministry how she does it, I cringe. Two words are always the predictable answer: *diet* and *exercise*. Were you hoping this subject wouldn't come up? We're told in the Bible that how we manage our body affects our ministries and the quality of our lives. The apostle Paul put it this way: "I discipline my body and bring it into subjection, lest, when I have preached to others, I myself should become disqualified" (1 Corinthians 9:27). If your goal is a quality of life filled with quality days of serving the Lord, attention to your body is key!

Father, the human body is so complex and intricate. What amazing creatures You created! Because I want to be a good steward of the body You gave me, I'm going to start exercising in some way and eating more nutritious foods. Please watch over me and guard my health. Amen.

Reading Promotes Growth

There was a time when reading was more popular than watching TV. Imagine that! Are you wondering, Who has time to read? Ruth Graham told her daughters, "Keep reading and you'll be educated!" It's easy to think you don't have time to read, but simply carrying a book everywhere you go gets many books read. I used to set my timer and read for just five minutes a day. It may not sound like much, but I've gone through many books this way! Reading can play an important role in your spiritual growth. Of course the Bible is the primary book you should read, but the books of women such as Ruth Graham, Edith Schaeffer, Elisabeth Elliot, and Anne Ortlund are also good. When you read their books, you are being mentored!

God, as I read my Bible this week, open my eyes so I can grasp Your wisdom and principles for life. Help me incorporate them into my life. And also lead me to books that will help me love You and the people around me more thoroughly. Amen.

God's Timing

I'm tempted at times to think my quiet time with God doesn't matter. That it doesn't count. Nobody sees it, and sometimes it feels like there's no glory, no attention given to the weeks, months, and years of waiting on God. Can you relate? After all, few people, if any, see you reading God's Word. No one's there to watch you memorize and meditate on God's life-changing truths.

Let me encourage you! God sees you on bended knee in prayer. He uses your dedication and openness to prepare you for ministry. And He will present those opportunities in His time. Right now, you're responsible for cooperating with God's efforts to prepare you. So clear your calendar. Set aside some time to place yourself before God. Wait on Him!

God, today I pray Psalm 119:27 to You: "Make me understand the way of Your precepts; so shall I meditate on Your wonderful works." Open my eyes and my heart to Your wisdom, Father, and give me Your directions today. Amen.

Be All There

Wherever you are, be all there! Live life to the hilt in every situation you believe to be the will of God. Go expecting God to use you. Go to give, to reach out. Withhold nothing. Be what one woman calls a "hanger-arounder." As long as you've already set aside the time and made the effort to go to an event, give totally and freely. Minister to as many people as you can in as many ways as you can. It's a surefire way to glorify and serve God! A friend and I have made a pact: When we find ourselves gravitating toward each other at an event or a party, one of us will announce: "C'mon! Let's go touch some sheep."

Lord, I want to tell everyone what a wonderful God You are. If I'm tired, give me strength. If I'm feeling shy, give me courage. If I'm hesitant, give me the right words to say. Thank You. Amen.

Memorizing God's Word

Want a great way to honor God? Memorize His Word! Before you say it, let me just tell you: It's never been easy for me either. I was in a friend's home and their parrot sang *Jingle Bells*…in its entirety! As I stood there amazed at what I was hearing, I thought, Well if a parrot can learn *Jingle Bells,* I can memorize Scripture! Think of the time it took for someone to sit with that bird and teach it the melody and words of a song. Surely you can learn a verse or two from God's Word. If you do, your filled heart will be a source of encouragement to many!

Lord, turn on my brain and help me absorb Your Word today. And then give me the desire and gumption to put Your wisdom and precepts into practice and share them with others. Amen.

Showing Mercy

Is there someone who could use your encouragement today? A loved one? Someone who's away from family and friends? Mercy is a quality that's required of us if we're going to love and serve God. And it's something we're uniquely equipped to do as women. After all, our Lord Jesus modeled it for us so many years ago, and we're to follow in His steps. Commit now to rekindle your efforts to show mercy and to serve others with all your heart. Matthew 5:7 reads, "Blessed are the merciful, for they shall obtain mercy."

Lord, give me a heart of compassion. Help me notice the needs of people around me and discover how I can ease their burdens, even if it's only in small ways. I want to reflect Your love and care to them. Amen.

Choices

The importance of choices cannot be overestimated. If you want to know what you'll be like in the future, check out the choices you're making today. What you're doing now, so you will be then. It's something of a riddle. Over time your choices change…for the better, I hope! The choices you make right now will determine whether or not you fulfill God's design for your life. Whatever you're dealing with right this minute, the next five minutes, the next hour, tomorrow, or forever—make positive decisions to love, honor, and serve the Lord. Make the choices that will alter your world…and the lives of others in positive ways.

Lord, every time I turn around I have to make decisions. Should I get up? Should I eat this or that? Should I discipline my kids? Should I buy this? Should I volunteer for this project? Please give me guidance so I will choose Your path and do Your will. Amen.

One Day at a Time

"Be calm. All you have to do is take one day at a time." I remind myself of this quite often as I look at my planner. How about you? Do you just let things happen? Many people do. And then they wonder why God doesn't seem to use them in effective ministry. To get control in your life is going to take some careful planning. Take life one day at a time. Use a day planner or something similar. Map out the next day's appointments, meetings, menus, and carpool assignments.

Tonight, when you slip under the covers, ask God to bless the next day and guide you through it. Then turn off the light. In the morning welcome the day with the psalmist's words of praise: "This is the day the LORD has made; [I] will rejoice and be glad in it!" (118:24).

Lord, You've given me today. I want to enjoy doing Your will every minute. Psalm 119:105 says Your Word is a lamp unto my feet. Thank You for showing me Your ways. Amen.

Your Priorities Are Showing

What do your calendar, "to do" list, weekly commitments, and even your checkbook register say about you? What do they suggest about your walk with God? About your priorities? Take a look. Is it time to line up your priorities based on what you believe and not on the desires and whims formulated by what you see and hear via people and advertising?

Prayerfully consider what changes you need to make to set your priorities on what you believe about God and His call to service. Psalm 90:12 says, "Teach us to number our days, that we may gain a heart of wisdom." A heart of wisdom! That's exactly what you need as you live the priorities you hold dear.

Lord, I'm so easily swayed by advertising and wanting what other people have. Every time I'm ready to spend money, remind me that You are my priority...and that You provide my income so I can serve You, provide for my family, and promote Your kingdom. Amen.

Life's Often Unfair

Are you feeling like life is unfair? Let me encourage you. When I think of the women of great faith I know, I can almost always point to some sorrow or tragedy that's caused them to have a growing trust in God. A widow who lost her young husband, a writer who writes from her bed because of a disease she'll never get over, a mother who lost a child in a tragic accident, a woman who suffers with cancer.

What's lacking in your life, my friend? I know what's lacking in mine. But I'm giving praise to God for His unfailing loving-kindness and all-sufficient grace. It's what keeps me sane and happy and healthy. And it will do the same for you!

Lord, I don't understand why people have to endure hardships and tragedies. Sometimes I get scared thinking about what could happen. But You are here for me. You will give me the strength and courage I need to persevere. Thank You. Amen.

Prayer for Patience

Contrary to the adage, "Don't pray for patience because God will give you situations that require it," asking for patience is a good thing! These uplifting words in Romans 8:28 tell us we can "know that all things work together for good to those who love God." God is in control of everything—even those situations that appear negative. And He will work those out for your good and for His purposes. So don't be afraid to pray for patience. God will see you through...and you'll acquire this wonderful fruit of the Spirit!

I love the greeting card that says, "Bloom where you're planted!" As God cultivates your soil, adds growth enhancers, plants, and prunes unnecessary branches, rejoice. Someday you'll say with confidence, "Sure enough, God worked all things together for His good purposes!"

Father, patience is a virtue, I know. Help me nurture this trait so I can better reflect You and wait on Your timing. Thank You for willingly taking the time to develop my character so I can better serve You. Amen.

When We're Asked to Pray

Are you praying for your friends? Really praying? I have to say, not much in life compares in importance—or in emotion—to what's going on in the lives of the people I love. When my father was dying from cancer, I cared very little about world news, the latest books, or anything else for that matter. Somehow things like that don't matter in times of crises. Being followers of Jesus means listening to people and then praying diligently for them. Who are the family members you regularly bring before God in prayer? Who are the friends? Paul's words to the Philippians echo in us too: "I have you in my heart" (Philippians 1:7). Lift a prayer for your family and friends today.

Lord, when You walked on the earth and people brought their sick or paralyzed friends to You, You healed them. Help me to always bring my friends and family members to You in prayer. Amen.

Getting into the Word

Trust me. Just about everything and anything can keep you from getting into God's Word. Maybe it's the little ones underfoot. Or maybe it's your job. There just isn't time to stop before you dash out the door. Or maybe you just never seem to get around to it! What are your greatest obstacles to spending time alone with God? Sit down and write out what you can—and will—do to find a lifestyle pattern that includes Bible study. Talk to friends about their schedules. Find out ways they enjoy God's Word. Make a prayer list. My desire is that you'll develop passion for God's Word. That you will truly be a dedicated and growing follower of Jesus.

Lord, Your Word is such a treasure! I want to hide it in my heart, to let it dwell richly within me, to use it to guide every decision I make. Thank You for speaking to me through the pages of the Bible. Amen.

Words of Kindness

Kind words are short to speak, but their echoes are endless. Dig around in your heart. Expose any problem areas. Do you need to confess and admit to the sin of gossip? Do this each and every time you gossip. Are you dealing with hatred? Foolishness? Idleness? Be honest. As women, let's make godly speech a lifetime goal. We want to follow in the footsteps of Jesus, whose lips spoke words of love and kindness. Let's make this our constant prayer as it was David's—"I will guard my ways, lest I sin with my tongue" (Psalm 39:1). How wonderful to aspire to godly speech! In fact it's our mandate if we're going to truly follow God.

Lord, may my speech always be gracious. Help me not to let any unwholesome talk come out of my mouth, but only what is helpful for building others up according to their needs. Amen.

10 Ways to Love Your Children

There's nothing more important than the value of spending as much time as possible with our children. We have the awesome privilege and joy of loving them and molding them in godly directions. In this brief devotion there are 10 ways to love your children! 1) Teach them and train them. 2) Do not provoke them (Ephesians 6:4). 3) Talk to God about your kids. 4) Talk to them about God. 5) Read up on mothering. 6) Read to them. 7) Teach them to pray. 8) Take care of them. 9) Tell them about Jesus. 10) Do your best to model godliness.

A very wise person said, "If we don't set aside ungodliness today—it'll show up in our children tomorrow."

Lord, I love my children! Help me care for them just as You care for me—consistently, compassionately, and creatively. Amen.

Love Your Neighbor

"I can't say I know her that well. You know how it is. I'm busy. Anyway, she's not my type." Can you relate to this attitude? We can't read very far in the New Testament without discovering that to be a Christian means to love your husband, love your children, and love one another...including your neighbors. Ouch! As children of God, you and I, my friend, are commanded to show the kind of love we see modeled by our heavenly Father. The command is clear in John 15:12: "Love one another as I have loved you." As you spend time in God's Word, you're going to find the best instruction there is about what love looks like. And loving your neighbor is definitely part of God's plan.

Lord, I admit that sometimes I don't even notice the hurting people around me. I pray for sensitivity so I can see other people's needs and know how I can help. Amen.

Committed to Love

Have you ever done or said or implied that your love for your husband is conditional or even waning? Loving your husband is a 24-hours-a-day job. Scripture says simply, "God is love" (1 John 4:8 and 16). And since we have God in us, His love is in us. That's what enables you to love when you don't feel like it. To serve when you'd rather be served. True, sacrificial love comes only from God. "God so loved the world that He gave His only begotten Son" (John 3:16). Jesus didn't come to be served but to serve (Mark 10:45). It was on purpose; it was deliberate that He died for you and me on the cross (Luke 22; Romans 14:8-9). Ask Him to fill you with strong, steadfast, lasting love for your husband.

Lord, on my own I can't even begin to love my husband as consistently and sacrificially as You want me to. Fill me to overflowing with Your love every day so I can serve from a full heart and never run dry. Amen.

I Can Do This

"I can't do this! And you can't expect me to. It's way more than I bargained for!" When I'm facing difficult or painful times, I pray: "God, Your Word says I can do all things—including handling this—through Christ who strengthens me. By Your grace, I can do this. Thank You for enabling me to meet the challenge!" (Philippians 4:13). Don't get me wrong, I'm no spiritual giant. I'm just a woman who wants God to enable her to meet the challenges of life head-on. With this prayer I'm acknowledging the incredible resources I have in the Lord. It allows me to march right through what lies before me…to truly follow Jesus. My prayer is that you'll not give in or give up. By His grace!

Lord, my resources are so limited. I often feel small and weak. But You are strong! Thank You for giving me the power I need to accomplish everything You ask me to do. Amen.

True Joy

"I thought once I became a Christian I'd be happy. But this isn't working for me!" Our lives are filled with disappointments, crises, afflictions, and struggles. But there's good news. God can give us all the joy we need. True spiritual joy is not necessarily happiness. Happiness comes and goes depending on our circumstances. If all's well, we're happy. But as soon as things get hectic or there's a tragedy, happiness becomes very elusive. God's joy is a gift of grace for the hardships and the problems of life. It's supernatural joy. And it's not dependent on circumstances because it's based on God's never-changing, unconditional love for us. We need to look beyond the hard times and know that all is well between us and the Lord.

Lord, even my most difficult situations can't take away the joy You give me—if only I will look to You. Thank You that Your joy gives me strength. Amen.

Money Managing

"That was the bank. We're overdrawn again!" That was my Jim talking to me! I was a carefree, uninformed wife who threw up her hands and said, "Oh, I don't know anything about money. I let Jim take care of all of that." That might sound like the epitome of trust, but that attitude actually represented ignorance, foolishness, and immaturity. If you understand financial matters, find ways to contribute. Take some of the load off your husband. I finally decided to be more active in this area, so I talked to Jim, solicited advice from knowledgeable people, and read books on basic accounting. I encourage you to bone up on money management. Start some kind of record-keeping system. I know this isn't very glamorous, but your contribution in the financial arena develops virtue, character, godliness, and yes, spiritual beauty.

Lord, You call us to be good stewards, and I want to do my part. Give my husband and me wisdom as we make financial decisions together. Show us how to please You with the resources You give us. Amen.

Look to God

What trial is causing you the greatest grief, the sharpest pain, the deepest sorrow today? Is it an unbelieving husband? The loss of a job? The breakup of your marriage? A prodigal child? Loneliness? Whatever your greatest trial, let it move you to God. Hebrews 13:15 encourages you to faithfully offer to God the sacrifice of your praise. Do this even if it's through your tears. Jesus gives us the supreme model of joy in the midst of life's dark pain. There was no greater pain than crucifixion on a Roman cross. But the Lord never lost His joy in the relationship He had with His Father. He even endured the cross. Lift your eyes and heart to the Lord today. Give Him your thanks and praise as you seek His help and comfort.

Lord, may every circumstance in my life move me closer to You. Help me lift my eyes off my problems and onto You so I will always rejoice in You. Amen.

Turning Your Thoughts Godward

"I'm doing just fine." When you hear that do you wonder if the person is telling the truth? Have you answered this way when it's not true? I used to hide my pain. My thoughts pulled me down so far that, in private, tears streamed down my cheeks. How did I counter these sorrows? I kept going back to Philippians 4:8: "Whatever things are true...meditate on these things." I contemplated the truth about God's love and the truth about God's promises. They are constant and never fail.

It's not always easy to shift focus from the situation and onto God, to dwell on what is true. But to live a victorious Christian life, you must do what the Word says. God is at work to help you accomplish whatever He's asking you to do. Trust Him.

Lord, You have given me so many wonderful things I can focus my attention on. Help me to delight in the good things You have put in my life. Give me discernment so I can know the truth and cling to it. Amen.

A Loser

When you feel worthless or like a failure, remember you are a child of God! Ephesians 2:10 calls you His workmanship. From one woman to another, I want you to be encouraged that God has a grand plan and purpose for your life. Oh, you may not feel it right now, but God is faithful and always keeps His promises. He says, "For I know the thoughts that I think toward you...thoughts of peace and not of evil, to give you a future and a hope. Then you will call upon Me and go and pray to Me, and I will listen to you. And you will seek Me and find Me, when you search for Me with all your heart. I will be found by you, says the LORD" (Jeremiah 29:11-14). Now that's something you can count on!

Lord, help me see myself as You see me. Not more, not less. Just the person You created with a specific plan and purpose all my own. Thank You for hope and the future You have in mind for me. Amen.

If Only…

"If only I had taken that job. Maybe I'd be able to do some of the things I've always wanted to do." If only…if only…if only. This kind of thinking is counterproductive to say the least. It's time to give that regret up! God calls us to deal with what is now. "If only" thinking usually makes us sad or depressed. It's impossible to change the past—so why live there? Learn from it, yes. See what God is teaching you and remember His faithfulness. And then move on. Acknowledge God's sovereignty over every event of your life—past, present, and future. Thank Him for the opportunities still to come and look for the possibilities He'll bring into your life so you can achieve your dreams. God loves you!

Lord, thank You that I don't have to be haunted by "if only." You guide me to places of amazing possibilities. As I love You and walk with You, I know those moments will be there. Help me be ready for them. Amen.

Time Alone with God

"Prayer and quiet time? I'm lucky to get five minutes to myself for a shower every day." I'm so sympathetic! And yet when we don't take time alone with God, we're in danger of losing the very best that people desire from us. In His quiet time alone with God before the sun rose, Jesus acquired focus for the day (Mark 1:35). He let it shape His plans. Take some moments of stillness to discover God's plan for your day. Then by the time your family gets up, the phone rings, or you get into the car, you have His direction to guide you. I know it's not easy. And there are days when it just won't happen. But when it does, you'll be there to reap the rewards and be prepared to meet the challenges to come.

Lord, meeting with You at the beginning of my day restores my soul. I love that You love our time together too. Help me make being with You a priority for each new morning. Amen.

Attitude Helpers

I've been experimenting over the years with what I call my "attitude helpers." In my desire to be and do all God calls me to, this list has helped on more than one occasion. 1) Pray for those you serve and for yourself. 2) Pray specifically about your attitude toward your work. 3) Make a list of verses that encourage you in joy. 4) Do your work unto the Lord. 5) Tackle each task creatively. 6) Be energetic. 7) Look for the benefits—this will lighten your load. 8) Value each day— one step at a time.

How will you live today? How closely will you walk with God? Incorporate these attitude helpers into your life. When you choose to live with a willing, happy heart, you become a source of God-given joy to all!

Lord, my attitude, though seated in my heart, shows up in my face and voice. I pray that both my expressions and tone will reflect that You are my Lord today as I joyfully obey and follow You. Amen.

Early to Bed, Early to Rise

If you're always running behind, why not cultivate the discipline of getting up early? Do I hear a groan? Well, I'm not a morning person either. Figure out what time you want to have things completed in your planning, in your prep for the day, and then work backward. That's the time you need to get up. And as you turn out the light tonight, center your thoughts on what you desire to accomplish for the Lord. Think of all the life you are "buying back" by getting up early. The time you spend praying and planning in the early part of the day gives you a master plan that works. Up and at 'em! Approach your day with energy and enthusiasm.

Lord, I love our time together, and I want to make a place for it early in the day. That will help me redeem other aspects of my day more fully. Thank You for the strength and wisdom You give me each day. Amen.

Getting the Job Done

I smile when I think about a housekeeping survey I conducted. I asked 100 women, "What keeps you from getting your housework done?" Their answers? Poor use of time. Lack of motivation. Failure to plan. And plain ol' procrastination. Sounds right, doesn't it! When I had no goals—or unclear ones—I was unmotivated.

But now I've changed, although I still fall back into old habits every once in a while. After an in-depth study of the Proverbs 31 woman, I decided to put her virtues into action in my life. She knew her goals and was aware she was on assignment from God to build a home. That's great motivation! She worked hard and was focused so God used her mightily. Whew!

Join me in seeking to become a better servant to God and the people we love!

Lord, it's so easy to focus on myself. Help me overcome that. Great joy can be found in loving and serving others. I want to excel in those things as I seek daily to please You. Amen.

Night Work

What do you do in the evenings? Do you watch TV? Surf the Internet? I encourage you to make your evenings and weekends count. I shudder to think what I'd be doing (or not doing!) if I'd continued to throw away God's gift of evenings. One Sunday at church I walked right past a friend of mine. She'd lost 40 pounds so I didn't recognize her. She grabbed my arm to get my attention. She told me she'd set a goal to find a new, uplifting activity she could do in the evenings. So she started exercising every night after work. And what a payoff! I was inspired to make my evenings more productive. I encourage you to whisper a prayer to God, asking Him to guide your heart and hands toward a little diligent night work.

Lord, between the end of the afternoon and before I lay my head down on my pillow, I want the hours to count for something. Thank You for the evenings. Help me use this time in a way that pleases You. Amen.

Getting a Handle on Goodness

If you want to be known as a woman who loves God and serves others, it starts with a goodness that's only possible through God's grace. One Bible teacher describes goodness as "the sum of all God's attributes." Wouldn't it be great if people walked out their doors every day ready to do good...even looking for chances to do so? Goodness takes the step from intentions to active serving. The Bible says, "Therefore, as we have opportunity, let us do good to all, especially to those who are of the household of faith" (Galatians 6:10). Dear friend, look for ways to bless people. Humble yourself in prayer as you seek ways to serve. Shine forth God's glory as you bear the fruit of goodness (Galatians 5:22).

Lord, goodness is a fruit of the Spirit. Help me reap a great harvest of this crop in my life. I know it will benefit me, but it will also touch other lives with a bit of heaven. Thank You for Your goodness. Amen.

A Woman of Focus

"I'm going to say no. It's a wonderful project, but just not where I'm going with my life right now." Can you imagine yourself saying this? When you have a sense of God's call on your life, you're focused. You know where you're going. You have direction. And believe me, it makes it a lot easier to make decisions. If you don't sense this strong call, rivet your attention to God's Word. Ask God to show you what He has for you to do. When He answers, you'll find it is much easier to say no to "opportunities" that don't fit your priorities or time constraints. You'll also have more time and energy to commit to the options that are right for you. Make all you do count for the Lord.

Lord, I pray that I would look neither right nor left when I'm following You. I don't want to be distracted, even by good things. I want to save my time and energy for the best things You are calling me to. Amen.

An Exciting Time with God!

Have you thought about your life's purpose? Take some time by yourself as soon as you can. Close the door and spend 60 uninterrupted minutes with God. I guarantee you won't be the same after this hour with your Lord! After praising Him, pray about His goals for your life. Write them down. Seeing them in black and white will be very motivating. Select from your list the three that are most significant to you. Rank them in order of importance. Now, as you go through the next few days, ponder these goals. Jot down ways you can achieve them, including specific steps to take. You'll discover new dimensions to your life and new energy for God's calling.

Lord, as I commit these minutes to You, please give me Your goals and dreams for my future. What are the good works You've prepared for me? Show me, Lord. I'm willing. Amen.

How Do You Spell "Love"?

"I haven't had any time since my baby was born" is a common refrain. Be encouraged, Mom! You're doing the work of ministry big-time. "Love" is spelled:

T-I-M-E.

A lifetime of time to be exact. Did you know that 50 percent of a child's character and personality development takes place by age three? And our children need our time when they're becoming young adults in junior high and high school. When our kids are even older...adults themselves, they need our time and they're ready to be our friends. Of the woman in Proverbs 31, it says her children rise up to bless her. Parenting is an incredible privilege! Give your children all the time and resources they need to succeed and become the people God created them to be.

Lord, I'm tired...but I'm a mom! Renew my strength as I love the precious gifts You've given me. Give me wisdom to care for them, kindness in my discipline, and love in every minute we're together. Amen.

Be Faithful

Faithfulness is a major distinction of a Christian woman, and it's a quality God is looking for (1 Timothy 3:11). A godly woman comes through... no matter what. She offers no excuses because she delivers the goods. She keeps her word. She shows up early and sticks to her commitments. She doesn't neglect worship, and she's devoted to duty. Does that sound too hard to follow? Ask God to cultivate His faithfulness in your life.

Now take a quick inventory of your life. What areas do you excel in? What areas do you need to improve in? Lift your heart and desire before the Lord, praising Him for His faithfulness to you, and promising to be more faithful to Him. As the saying goes, "You may depend on the Lord, but can He depend on you?"

Lord, I have so much to be thankful for...and faithful over. I see areas that I've given to You...and I rejoice with You in those. But then there are those other areas...Help me to press on as I grow in You. Amen.

More Like Him

Have you ever noticed that the more you are with someone, the more you become like that person? If you've been married a while, you'll notice you and your husband use the same figures of speech. You share many of the same opinions and perspectives on life. You'll even see this principle at work in your children. And if you're single, you experience the same thing with your close friends and family. And it works the same way when it comes to God! The more time you spend reading the Bible, the more you resemble Him. You begin to think as God thinks and do what He would do. You desire what He desires. As you spend time with Him, your life takes in and reflects more and more of His love and glory. Commune with Him each day and spend time in His Word. You'll reap tremendous rewards!

Lord, I know You are with me always, but the special times we spend together are so life-giving. Thank You for Your Word and the light it gives on my journey. Amen.

Majoring on the Minors

So many people today have problems because they don't have a positive relationship with God. They get caught up in the day-to-day struggles and forget to look at the big picture. They major on the minors. What really counts in the Christian life is knowing God. This is foundational.

Sadly, we too often focus on meeting needs, providing support, and facilitating fellowship rather than promoting the God who gives us life and loves us so much. John 3:16-17 reminds us, "For God so loved the world that He gave His only begotten Son, that whoever believes in Him should not perish but have everlasting life. For God did not send His Son into the world to condemn the world, but that the world through Him might be saved." Don't forget to offer people the ultimate solution for their troubles!

Lord, help me turn to You first when I am struggling with a problem. Thank You that You always care for me. Remind me often that You have more for my life than only me. Amen.

Does God Really Care?

"God forgot about me a long time ago." Dear friend, nothing is further from the truth! I've heard women say, "But God doesn't care about me. He doesn't see how I'm being treated." I've said it myself, "Elizabeth, why don't you just quit now? Why try? Why bother?" Psalm 139:14 is a wonderful reminder that "I am fearfully and wonderfully made." Second Timothy 1:9 says God has a grand plan and purpose for my life. In Romans 8:35 Paul asks, "Who shall separate us from the love of Christ?" Dear friend, love God with all your mind. Do it by thinking true thoughts about yourself. You'll experience the joy and hope of being in close relationship with God through Jesus Christ. It's then you'll see yourself as God does— as His delightful creation.

Lord, sometimes I become so focused on myself that there's no room to see me from Your perspective. Help me turn my eyes to You and believe the things You say are true about me. Amen.

Sweet Encouragement

I urge you to share your spiritual journey with other women. A "group" provides you with personal care and interest. The sharing is delightful and uplifting. You'll have sisters-in-Christ who pray for you. You'll be able to exchange experiences. You'll have accountability. And, yes, even some peer pressure. That's not always a bad thing, you know. It helps me get a lot done, frankly. And there's sweet, sweet encouragement as you stimulate one another to greater love and greater works of love. Hebrews 10:24 says, "Let us consider one another in order to stir up love and good works." Growing in Christ is fun...but stretching. My greatest desire for you is that you become a woman who pleases God!

Lord, I love Hebrews 3:13, which says we are to encourage each other every day, as long as it's called "Today." Let me be an encourager to the women You've placed in my life. Amen.

As a Woman Thinks…

"You're always so grouchy." Ouch! That's where the rubber meets the road, isn't it? For years I was a prisoner of my dark moods, of my dark thoughts. I know all too well the frightening ability thoughts have to program our lives. Proverbs 23:7 is right in its message—whatever we think in our hearts, we are. But as I look back, I'm overwhelmed with gratitude to God for His wisdom. He provided help through His Word—the Bible. Words to help me develop a healthier thought life. Words to give me the effectiveness and energy to truly become a woman who reflects God's graciousness and joy. In times of depression and testing, fill your heart with what's true. Choose to love God with all your mind.

Lord, teach me Your truth! Fill me with Your thoughts as I read Your Word. Give me wisdom to understand what the Scriptures mean. Help me seek You with all my mind and never stop seeking You and loving Your Word. Amen.

Loving the Unlovely

Isn't it so much easier to love people who are gracious and mature? Oh, it's a cinch to love the lovely, but what about people who are hateful? Now that presents a challenge. In the Sermon on the Mount, Jesus shocked everyone by saying, "I say to you, love your enemies...for [God] makes His sun rise on the evil and on the good, and sends rain on the just and on the unjust" (Matthew 5:44-45). God's love is never deserved—it simply is! And that's the kind of love you and I are to extend to one another—whether people are rude, ungracious, or unlovely. God will give you the grace and the strength you need!

God, You chose to love me regardless of my faults, failures, and sin. You delight in me and direct me to the good actions You've already prepared for my life. I want to reflect You to others today. Amen.

Why Worry?

"It's one-thirty and here comes Linda. She's on time today because I told her lunch was at one o'clock." Have your friends ever done this with you? With a little planning, they won't have to trick you anymore. I keep on track by making a "to do" list for everything imaginable. As I prepare and plan, I also pray. I give God everything, beginning with me. Doing this relieves some of the pressure of my day. I have a bookmark in my Bible that reads, "God is ready to assume full responsibility for the life yielded to Him." That's the secret of growing in Him. Of becoming all you can be. As I give God my home, my possessions, my time, I make headway. Try this process!

God, thank You for giving me a mind to use—to prepare and plan with. Right now I give my mind to You so my plans and preparations for today will show I trust You to care for me. Amen.

Sacrificial Love

Love is not the "stuff" you read about in magazines. Far from it! Love is something you do, not just something you feel. Let me encourage you. When you and I go before the Lord in prayer, He'll show us where He'd like us to love more sacrificially. He'll remind us that we're to obey Him as we walk in His steps and love one another—even when we don't feel like it! The Bible says, "Love is patient" and "kind" (1 Corinthians 13:4 NASB). With God's help, we can do this. As we look to God to empower us, pray the prayer of St. Francis of Assisi: "O Divine Master, grant that I may not so much seek to be loved—as to love."

Father, I kneel before You now. Please reveal to the eyes of my heart a little more of the love You demonstrated when You gave Your Son. Help me rest in that love and love others in the same way. Amen.

A Quality of Joy

Genuine joy—one that's rooted in Jesus Christ—is an expression of godliness. Does that surprise you? That quality of joy is a sure sign of God in your life. And there are some great reasons to be joyful. Maybe these reminders will lift your spirits today. In John 16:22 Jesus says that no one takes your joy away from you. That's great news! And because it's rooted in Christ, your joy is always available. That's why the Bible says you can "rejoice in the Lord always" (Philippians 4:4). Whatever the circumstances of your life, you have immediate access to God—the source of true joy—anytime, anyplace.

"Joy is the quality of life you have when you're with someone who loves you unconditionally." Lord, I'm so glad that's You! I'm glad You are in my life. Help me remember this moment by moment and revel in it. Amen.

A Family Designed by God

My heart grieves when I hear teenagers...or anybody, for that matter...say they hate their families. The family unit was designed by God. So how can you improve your family relationships? One thing is to give your kids the powerful benefit of seeing a healthy marriage. It's a legacy that can't be duplicated. But even if things aren't ideal, you can still bless and instruct your children. Create a pleasant home environment by living out your leadership role as a mother. Colossians 3:23 is such a wonderful passage: "Whatever you do, do it heartily, as to the Lord and not to men." Write that verse down and look at it as you begin your day. And don't forget your most powerful resource of all—prayer.

Father, You came up with the very idea of "family." You've made me Your child out of Your deep love. Please let me have Your attitude toward my own family today. Amen.

Keep Your Eyes Open

There are plenty of people around you in need. How can you help? Purchase double groceries and share them with a struggling couple, a single-parent family, or a widow. Clean out your wallet when an offering is taken for a special cause. Prepare a special meal for a woman having chemotherapy. Or pass along your children's clothes to a young family who's short of cash. Stop by and chat for a few minutes with the elderly lady next door. It doesn't take a lot to make a huge difference in someone's life. To reap the blessings that come with a ministry of giving, you've got to keep your ear to the ground and seize opportunities.

Lord, give me new ears for today. And give me eyes that don't look inward at my own concerns but look outward to others—in the same way Your eyes of love looked down on me and saw my need. Amen.

Seasons of Life

"I noticed Mom could barely hear us at dinner this weekend. Since Dad died she's never been quite the same." I can so identify with this woman. I've walked through several seasons of life myself. My dad died and my mother was institutionalized all within a few months. And yet during those days I also welcomed my first two grandbabies...one month apart!

Like you, I need God's promises for the seasons I'm experiencing as well as those to come. Isn't it wonderful that God's care is unceasing? His love unending? His guidance unfailing? And His presence everlasting? Absolutely! He is with us, dear friend, through every day, every situation, every relationship, every season. What a joy to know we're cared for by such a great God.

You are "the God who is there," Lord. Right now I can't see the end of this season in my life, but because You are here, I can make it through today. Thank You! Amen.

Preparing, Planning, Praying

Whatever the challenge, the task, the trial, or the crisis, God will provide for you, my dear sister in Christ. Philippians 4:19 promises that God will provide what we need. The wonderful fact is that when God commands us to do something, He also enables us to obey! You can discover that truth for yourself. Step out in trust as you walk through your day with the Lord. Not a day will go by without you experiencing His care. Think of it as the "three P's"— preparing, planning, and praying. God will help you meet the emotional, physical, and mental challenges today will bring.

Manna, Father. Every day You provided that food but the children of Israel had to go out of their tents and gather it. Help me, Father, look to You for provision and then step out in trust. Amen.

Don't Be Anxious

Jesus said, "Do not worry about tomorrow, for tomorrow will worry about its own things" (Matthew 6:34). If your life is uncertain and fraught with difficulties, be encouraged! God isn't asking you to handle your entire life all at once. More often than not your "what if" imaginings about the future turn out altogether differently. I encourage you to concentrate on today. With God's strength and grace, you'll make it. Choose to draw near to the God who loves you, who promises to care for you, and who loves you unconditionally. Let today be the boundary for your fears and emotions. Take life one day at a time. Okay, make it a half-day at a time! Isn't that what being a follower of Jesus is all about?

"Worry is a misuse of the imagination." Oh, Father, how those words fit me! So often I fill my imagination with "what ifs." Instead, help me to keep on being filled with the Spirit today so I can walk close to You. Amen.

Forget the Past

The past makes us what we are, but that's no reason to live there. Philippians 3:13-14 is a breakthrough passage of Scripture: "Forgetting what is behind and straining toward what is ahead, I press on toward the goal to win the prize for which God has called me..." (NIV). Poring over the disappointments and failures you experience will make you tired and depressed. And it's definitely a breeding ground for bitterness. Instead, open yourself to God's grace, to the excitement of living today. Reach forward. Press on. Forget about the past. Look to your glorious future with Christ!

Lord, thanks to You, my past is cleansed and taken care of. My present is where You are right now. And my future is with You, and I will see You as You are. This makes me want to get up and get going! To press on! Amen.

Forgiving Others

As Jesus hung on the cross He prayed, "Father, forgive them; for they do not know what they are doing" (Luke 23:34 NASB). When we fail to forgive others we sentence ourselves to a life of bitterness. Helen Roseveare was a missionary doctor brutally raped while serving in Africa. She forgave those who wronged her and spent 20 more years doing missionary service. Another outstanding woman of faith, Elisabeth Elliot, forgave the men who savagely killed her missionary husband. In fact, she continued in ministry to the very people who killed him. Ask God to shine His light in your darkness. Search out any bitterness and unforgiveness and turn it over to Him. You'll be glad you did.

Lord, help me to be an excellent forgiver...even when it's hard. Show me anyone against whom I've unknowingly held hard feelings. I forgive them just as You have so mercifully forgiven me. Amen.

Untiring Activity

Without purpose in your life—without goals that energize you to be all God wants you to be—you just "count days." Is that really what you want? Become a woman of untiring activity. God's grace will keep you from being a breathless, harried, frazzled female. I love the promise of Isaiah 40:31: "Those who wait for the LORD will gain new strength; they will mount up with wings like eagles, they will run and not get tired, they will walk and not become weary" (NASB). Living for Christ means going all the way to the end with purpose and enthusiasm. God's in control. Rest in Him.

Lord, I thank You for the promise of new strength, of wings like eagles, and the energy to run and not get tired. When I get tired, remind me gently of Your provision for all the strength I need to go on, full of purpose and enthusiasm. Amen.

A Lack of Trust

When you start taking matters into your own hands, it's clear evidence of not trusting God. Remember, God knows what is going to happen (Psalm 139:16). And He will enable you to cope and grow even in hard times. He literally works good from bad. Remember the story of Joseph? His brothers sold him into slavery, but many years later Joseph was able to help his family. He told his brothers that what they meant for evil, "God meant it for good, in order to bring it about as it is this day, to save many people alive" (Genesis 50:20). It's a truth found in Scripture, and I've seen it at work. Trust the Lord in your trials, and watch as He keeps His promises and uses the situations for His purposes.

Lord, it's hard to be thankful for trials. And yet You use them to bring positive change to my life. Help me see the next trial through eyes of faith. Give me Your peace as You use my trial as a growth opportunity. Amen.

The Morning Prayer

Begin your day by choosing to follow God's ways all day long. Pray and purpose to do His will every minute. Yes, even with those phone calls you'd rather not take, the meetings you'd rather skip, the meals you'd rather not cook. My "morning prayer" helps keep me alert to God as I go about my day. It sets me up to successfully face the challenges along the way. And you know, it will also help you experience joy and peace as you go through your day. Throughout the day when you feel harried or overbooked, talk to God. You could say, "Please, God, let me respond in Your way. Help me stay calm. Help me know when to speak and when to listen. Help me to help!"

Lord, each day is so full of activity. Please help me keep focused on You throughout the day. I want to face each challenge with Your joy and peace. Keep me calm amid every storm. Amen.

God's Masterpiece

If you're like me, you want results right now! But patience and diligence pay off. One day a huge cube of marble was delivered to Michelangelo's studio. He walked around it, looking at it closely and touching it. Suddenly he grabbed a chisel and swung at the stone, causing chips of marble to fly in every direction. His apprentice yelled above the noise, "What are you doing? You're ruining a perfect piece of marble." Michelangelo answered, "I see an angel in there, and I've got to get him out." Whether this story is true or false, the principle is monumental. God looks at you and says, "I see someone who loves Me and wants to serve Me...a woman I can use to help others. I've got to get her out!" You were made in the image of Christ, and He wants to set you free.

Lord, sometimes I look at my life and see a hunk of raw marble. Thank You that with each blow of Your divine chisel You are releasing the woman of faith You created me to be. Amen.

Goodness Verses

I want to share with you two of my "goodness verses." Psalm 84:11 says, "The LORD will give grace and glory; no good thing will He withhold." James 1:17 reveals, "Every good and perfect gift is from above" (NIV). Memorize one or both of these goodness verses so you'll be prepared when life hits you between the eyes—and it will. God will use these scriptures for your comfort and to remind you of His presence. There's security in that, and it makes your faith real in your everyday life. Say this prayer today: "God, help me remember You are the Giver and the Protector." Consider His power and meditate on His promises. You will be blessed.

Lord, help me today to remember You are my Giver and Protector. You will withhold no good thing from me. You will not withhold Yourself from me…and You are indeed perfect goodness. Amen.

Trust God in the Dark

"Trust God in the dark." Those are the words of beloved author A.W. Tozer. And they're my encouragement to you today. I urge you not to get discouraged as you seek to grow. Trusting God is the perfect wisdom calling you to faith—no matter what. The truth is, you can eagerly exercise your will and faith in God when you know His wisdom stands behind all events, even the ones you don't understand. If you think about it, following God and living for Him is based on having full confidence in Him. Proverbs 16:20 is a great encouragement! "Whoever trusts in the LORD, happy is [she]."

Lord, it's hard to trust in the dark. I want to flip the light switch and see clearly. But You know the future, so I'm putting my faith in You. Help me walk steadily ahead, following Your light. Amen.

A Servant's Heart

Tape this over your kitchen sink or on the refrigerator door or at your desk: "True service is love in working clothes." Jesus said that He "did not come to be served, but to serve" (Mark 10:45). Put on those work clothes of love and serve your husband, your children, your extended family, and your friends. Every meal prepared, every piece of clothing washed, every room tidied, every visit, every act of doing for others is love in action. Married or single, you can exercise your servant heart wherever you are. There are always meals to take to those in need, Sunday school classes to teach, and people to encourage. Ask God to make your heart the heart of a servant.

Lord, cultivate within me a servant's heart. Open my eyes to the opportunities around me to serve others. May my every action for those around me be done with gladness and love. Amen.

Speak Up...but Not Always

There's a time to speak...and a time for silence. Knowing when to employ each is often the great challenge. I've struggled with this, and over the years I've had to learn—sometimes the hard way—that speaking and being silent also involve knowing the right timing and the right issues. Proverbs 20:18 reminds us, "By wise counsel wage war." How are you doing in this area? Do you know that when you choose to say something, how you say it is usually more important than what you say? Ask God to show you the right times to speak and the right times to be silent. Be very still while you wait for His answer. Wait patiently... then follow His advice.

Lord, help me speak with discernment. May the words of my mouth be chosen with care, and may I be alert for those times when it is better to stay silent. I pray You will be glorified in everything I say. Amen.

One Happy Fella

"How to Become the Woman of His Dreams!" How many magazine articles have you seen centered around this message? I can't guarantee you'll become your husband's ideal mate in every way, but if you meet God's standards for marriage, that husband of yours will be one happy fella! First, be a woman who fears the Lord. That's where true excellence is grown. Then love the Lord and obey His commands. Stay unshakably faithful to your marriage vows. Be glad when your husband is the center of attention. Cultivate fierce loyalty to him. Keep his shortcomings and failures to yourself. Be a positive emotional influence. Honor your husband daily and for life. Proverbs 12:4 calls that kind of woman "an excellent wife [who] is the crown of her husband."

Lord, thank You for the reminder that when I aim to fulfill Your design for marriage, I become a more excellent wife. Putting You first helps me put my husband first. May I take to heart what Your Word says to me as a wife. Amen.

A Prudent Woman

Prudent? It sounds so old-fashioned...but what a wonderful attribute for any woman to have. *Prudent* is exactly what Proverbs 19:14 calls the wife who is from the Lord: "Houses and riches are an inheritance from fathers, but a prudent wife is from the LORD." This wife is in a special category. She's a blessing to her husband directly from the hand of God. A husband is set for life with a wife like this. Replace the word *prudent* with *disciplined, reasoned, practical, delightful*...and you begin to get the picture. You are one of the Lord's greatest gifts to your husband!

And you don't have to be married to reap the rewards of being a prudent woman. You'll be blessed... and you'll be a delight to everyone around you.

Lord, teach me to be prudent. Help me exercise diligence, wisdom, and self-control in all I do. Though living prudently requires work on my part, I know the blessings to me and others make it worthwhile. Amen.

Resting in the Lord

"I'd love to do that for you, but I can't add one more thing to my schedule!" We've all either heard this, said this, or both. We never seem to have enough time, do we? How are you handling the pressures of life? With peace or panic? I liken our lives as women to a "hurricane of female hyperactivity." And that's not always a good thing. The fact is, when we're running around in circles, we're not doing as the Bible says when it calls us to "rest in the LORD" (Psalm 37:7). Is your relationship with Jesus your first priority? Or are you just too busy to sit at His feet and enjoy His presence? The woman whose heart and soul are at rest is the woman who embraces this truth of Scripture: Our times are in God's hands.

Lord, thank You for the gift of time. Help me use it in ways that honor and glorify You. Give me the wisdom to know when to let go of my schedule, concentrate on Your guidance, and help others. Amen.

Show Me

"I can't help it! I just know I'll fail, so why bother?" Does that sound like you today? Well, one sure way to face your fears is to equip yourself with the knowledge and assurance that comes from God's Word— from knowing His promises. This reminds me of my junior high algebra teacher who was from Missouri, the "Show Me" state. One of her teaching methods was to say, "Show me!" She wanted proof we knew what we were talking about. So cultivate your knowledge and faith in God's Word. This kind of wisdom and belief allows you to face your fears and show others where your strength and endurance come from. God is calling you to move out, conquer those fears, and share His provision. Can you hear Him? He's saying, "Show Me!"

Lord, You never meant for Your children to live in fear. That's why, in Your Word, You've given promises of strength, protection, and hope. May I take time to hide Your promises in my heart so I will no longer be afraid. Amen.

Search Me, O God

"There's nothing I'd like better than to put him in his place!" Hmmm…which weaknesses are most evident in your life? When was the last time you prayed this prayer of David found in the book of Psalms? "Search me, O God, and know my heart; try me, and know my anxieties; and see if there is any wicked way in me" (139:23-24). That's where the rubber meets the road, isn't it? Then what do you do? You need to confess what God reveals to you and submit to the transforming power of God's Holy Spirit. This means living each moment in submission to God. We please God with the thoughts we choose to think, the words we choose to say, and the actions we choose to take. Let God work in you today!

Father, I want to pray as David prayed—that You would reveal to me the condition of my heart. Help me be sensitive to Your transforming work within me so that my every thought, word, and action is pleasing to You. Amen.

No Expectations

When we're nice to someone, we automatically expect that person to be nice to us. And when this doesn't happen, look out! Interestingly, Jesus said to do good, but He also said to expect nothing in return (Luke 6:35). Loving without thought of personal reward can be extremely difficult. In my ministry I often hear, "Elizabeth, I've served my husband faithfully, but he never does anything in return." Is this how you feel? Or is there a friend you're always helping without receiving any thanks? The Bible says, "Through love serve one another" (Galatians 5:13). When you serve someone, you are serving the Lord. That kind of love is never self-seeking. Its only intent is to love as Jesus loved.

Father, may I be more generous with my love, not expecting anything in return. May my satisfaction come from growing to love others as You love them. And may I never take Your love for granted. Amen.

The Good News

"I don't think I can take one more disappointment." Oh, how I identify with that struggle! Real life is filled with disappointments, tragedies, heartaches, and just plain old struggles. And I get tired of it, just like you do. But then I remember the good news. God can give us the joy we need—just when we need it. Jesus wants our joy to "be full." It says so in John 15:11. When we depend on God in the middle of our suffering, we'll find the power we need to praise Him despite the pain. We can actually give thanks for His goodness even when things aren't so good! Thanks to the working of God's Spirit in us, we can become women who love God in every circumstance.

Father, Your Word makes the Good News abundantly clear—I can know joy even when life is difficult. Help me to not become so preoccupied with my problems that I lose sight of the many blessings You continue to bring into my life. Amen.

Patience Is a Virtue

Patience is a virtue. Unfortunately, it's not one I'm always able to pull off. But God's Word says, "Put on a heart of patience!" First Timothy 6:11 says, "Pursue righteousness, godliness, faith, love, patience, gentleness." Just as we cover ourselves every day by putting on clothes, we are to dress our spirits with patience. And here's the hard part. When we see faults in other people or when we're annoyed by them in any way and want to be critical and lash out, we're to employ patience. That's an important key to harmony in all relationships. And believe me, sometimes it takes all of God's strength to help me remain silent and do nothing. Can you relate? It takes God's transforming grace for me to be patient in all situations.

Lord, when "patience" comes up I immediately think, "Be careful what you ask for!" because patience is so hard to learn. But Your Word says patience is good. It's a sign of someone who loves and serves and grows in You. And that's me, Lord! Teach me patience. Amen.

Smoothing the Rough Edges

God commands us to be kind. It's as simple as that…but it can be so hard to implement. We all get into debates and have emotions that run hot. Realistically, I can't imagine a home or office that doesn't have moments of tense exchanges. We need to turn our negative energy into God's kind of grace and kindness. How do we begin? Love others more than ourselves. It'll take some practice, but with God's help through prayer, we can make it happen. When we genuinely care about someone, we pay attention. We get involved. And that person becomes more important to us. Will you join me in letting God soften our hearts and smooth our rough edges? He'll make us into women who can be kind and gracious in every situation!

Father, it's so easy for me to get upset when something I've worked on doesn't get done right. It's hard to not be in control 100 percent of the time. In fact, Lord, I'm not in control. You are! Help me remember that. Amen.

When You're Tempted

"It's flattering to have him pay attention to me. It's more than I can say for Brian. And lunch? What can it hurt?" If you're alive, you're tempted. That's a simple fact of life. That's why you and I need God's self-control every minute of every day. We need His help to resist our "urges" regardless of how innocent we'd like to think they are. "No" can be a hard word to say, but it's the key to self-discipline. The psalmist says, "I will set nothing wicked before my eyes" (Psalm 101:3). Pray over everything—your marriage, your work, your trials, your temptations. The good news is that you can claim God's power. You can walk by His Spirit. You can win the battle. Isn't that wonderful!

Father, I'm so thankful You're in my life. "I can resist anything except temptation" seems so true. But in 1 Corinthians 10:13 You promise to not give me more than I can bear without giving me a way of escape. I praise You! Help me do my part. Amen.

Innocent Talk?

Godliness and maliciousness don't go together. That's pretty obvious. But we women often get caught up in behavior that doesn't honor God. I'm talking about gossip. We hear something about someone and pass it on because it's funny, or entertaining, or interesting. We like to be the source of information. But gossip translates to slander, and biblically *slanderer* is used in reference to people such as Judas Iscariot, the man who betrayed Jesus. It's also a title used for Satan. That's not very good company to be in! James notes, "Out of the same mouth proceed blessing and cursing." Then he exclaims, "These things ought not to be so" (James 3:10). Let's make Psalm 19:14 our motto: "Let the words of my mouth and the meditation of my heart be acceptable in Your sight, O LORD!"

Lord, give me wisdom to know when to speak and when to stay silent. I want to honor You and also be a person who constantly uplifts and blesses others. Show me how I can share a kind word or encourage someone this week. Amen.

A Woman's High Calling

I'm so blessed to have many older women in my life. But I didn't really know just how blessed I was until I got a letter from a woman who has no one to look up to. No one to teach her and show her the way to godly living. No one to encourage her to pursue God's highest calling. Isn't that sad?

I hope and encourage you to commit your life to becoming one of God's precious "older" women in the Lord. And this applies to anyone spiritually younger than you, be it a year or ten or twenty. To be a teacher that imparts wisdom and encourages others is God's will for your life. It's one of God's highest callings. Share what is excellent, what is good. The person you're mentoring will be blessed…and you'll be blessed!

*Father, give me the confidence and outgoing spirit
I need to reach out to others in Your name to share
Your love and wisdom. Show me how to speak and
what to say. Amen.*

Do Something Special

"Hi, honey. I'm home!…Honey, are you here? I'm home…" Face it. If you don't pamper that husband of yours—someone else just might! Do something special every day for your man. One woman I know has hot chocolate ready each evening for her hubby. They share delicious cocoa and conversation. My daughter Courtney pampers her husband by keeping homemade chocolate chip cookie dough in her freezer so she can treat him to warm cookies and milk each night when he's home. (Are you sensing a theme?) I know these are little things, but they deliver a loud and yummy message: I love you! Pray for your guy daily. Count the ways you can pamper him. Be the woman of Proverbs 31, who enables her husband to rise to greatness and, in return, is blessed by him and her children.

Father, I get caught up in what the kids are doing, how my career is going, what I need to accomplish. I want to keep my eyes on the priorities You've given me: You, my husband, my family, my friends, and others. Amen.

Time to Regroup

"If you kids don't settle down you're grounded—for life!" I'll never forget the time Jim and I stopped by one of our daughters' houses. She'd given us a key so we wouldn't ring the doorbell in case the kids were asleep. Our daughter was on the couch with her Bible on her lap. The house looked like a tornado hit it! I think I even spotted spaghetti noodles hanging from a light fixture. She looked up and said, "You wouldn't believe what happened around here. The kids were awful. I just had to take a few minutes and ask God to remind me how much I love and wanted these children!"

I was so impressed and pleased. She had the sense to stop, leave things as they were, and look to the Lord for His patience and a quiet spirit. Remember to do that when your life turns topsy-turvy.

Lord, thank You for always being available for the little things and the big things. I love that I can come to You for comfort, strength, and peace. Amen.

Enthusiasm for Jesus

If you're a young mom, this God-ordained time with your children will make a difference—a tremendous difference—in their lives. Teach them and train them. It's crucial and something you're uniquely qualified to do. Talk to God about them. Do spiritual battle on their behalf. The world is tugging at our children's hearts, pulling them down and away from God. So take time to be with them. Share the Bible—children love to hear the stories of heroes and people who love God. Tell them about Jesus…about how He loves them and came to help them. Teach your sons and daughters to pray. And try your best—with the Lord's help—to model godliness. The most valuable gift you can give your family is a good example.

Father, help me show my husband and my children my enthusiasm for You. Through the joy I have in You, I want to draw them in…to spark in their hearts a passion for loving and worshipping You. Amen.

Wisdom and Understanding

"I wish I felt better about going back to work. We need the money, that's for sure, but I just don't feel good about it." Wisdom and understanding can be found in the Bible book of Proverbs. Wisdom weighs all the options and then makes the right decision: If I go back to work full-time, what'll happen to my marriage, my children, my family's home life, my involvement at church? If I spend our money on this, what happens next month? If I fail to discipline my children now, what's next? If I waste my time today, what happens to my goals? If I watch or read this, how will it impact my spiritual life? Making decisions based on future ramifications is a discipline that takes effort. But the reward is a more satisfying life filled with wisdom and love.

Lord, give me a heart that can discern the right paths to take, the right decisions to make, the right options to choose. Thank You for giving me Your Word as a perfect guide. Amen.

Know God

"If I could only be sure God knows what's going on—maybe then I would feel more at ease." Let me assure you that God does know what's going on! When you know your heavenly Father and trust His Word you can lead a life that glorifies and honors Him. Get to know God more intimately by spending time in His Word and by talking to Him. And as you grow to love God more completely—with your mind as well as your heart—you can say with the apostle Paul, "Oh, the depth of the riches both of the wisdom and knowledge of God! How unsearchable are His judgments and His ways past finding out!" (Romans 11:33). The more you realize how much God loves you, the easier it becomes to know, follow, and accept His will for your life.

Father, open my heart and my mind to the truths in Your Word. Reassure me that You're in charge and that You love me. Thank You for all You do for me. Amen.

God Knows and Cares

"God...are You there? Do You know my hurts, my dreams, my disappointments? Can You hear me?" If this is your prayer today, rest in the knowledge that God is listening. "Now this is the confidence that we have in Him, that if we ask anything according to His will, He hears us. And if we know that He hears us, whatever we ask, we know that we have the petitions that we have asked of Him" (1 John 5:14-15).

God knows your hurts, your wants, your needs. He understands you. The wonderful news is that you never have to say to God, "But You don't understand." You can be confident that when no one else knows, He does. You're not carrying your burdens alone! By God's grace, accept every event of your life knowing it is in the hands of an infinitely wise God who loves you as no one else does.

Father, it's so wonderful to know You hear me. I always have someone I can go to—someone who totally loves me. That's You! Amen.

Acceptance and Obedience

Do you remember your mother saying, "I know you don't understand, but trust me—it's good for you!" Even though that was frustrating to hear, usually it was true. In this life we won't always understand why things are the way they are. Newspapers and TV are full of reports about tragedies and pain and sorrow beyond our understanding. And when we constantly badger God we get frustrated and exhausted. As God says, "My thoughts are not your thoughts, nor are your ways My ways…" (Isaiah 55:8-9).

Does this mean we can never question God? No. But simply put, we need to trust and obey Him. We can rest in the fact that our heavenly Father possesses perfect wisdom and knowledge however mysterious life seems to us. Accepting—without answers—is one way to love God completely.

Father, I like to know what's happening. I want to see now what good You're going to bring about. But that's usually not Your plan. Help me trust You and be confident You are present and involved down here on earth. Amen.

Lesser Choices

Do you know someone who used to be really involved in church life or Christian endeavors but now she seldom participates? Does this describe you? Somehow, at some time, for some reason, God has taken secondary place. And any one of us can let this happen when we make "lesser" choices. Less time in God's Word and prayer. Less time serving. Less time with Christian friends. At the core of our hearts we need to be passionate for God and His Word. When we fail to purposefully and willfully develop and maintain this focus, we begin to spend our precious time and days on lesser activities. And that can lead to wandering off the path of God's purpose for our lives.

I encourage you to do whatever it takes to get your passion back! Immerse yourself in God's Word. Discover His will afresh in your life. Praise Him!

Father, renew my spirit. Fill me with Your love. Remind me of all You've done for me. Strengthen my desire and commitment to love, worship, and serve You. Amen.

The Busy Woman

"I've tried! But reading my Bible and praying every day just isn't possible with my schedule." I've said this...and I'm guessing you can relate too. I've found some keys that help me keep the discipline of Bible study and prayer. Maybe they'll help you too.

Refuse to skip a day of study. God's Word is at the heart of every woman who loves God...even busy women. Ask God to open your eyes and heart to His truths (Psalm 119:18). Make yourself accountable to Christian friends or find a diligent prayer partner. Get up early before everyone makes demands on your time. Something is better than nothing, but always aim for more!

I can do this, Lord. I can dedicate some time every day to learning more about You. Keep distractions from me. Show me ways to isolate myself so I can focus completely on You. Amen.

First Things First

A "flashlight under the covers" book. Have you ever heard this expression about books people are highly recommending? There are a lot of books out there...some bad, some good, and some better. Make it a rule to read what honors God's standards and glorifies Him. And if you only have time to read one book, choose the Bible. Even if you have time to read to your heart's content, make God's Word the first book you read every day. Commit to no newspaper, no devotional, and no novel until your Bible is read. Be a woman of "the Book"! No matter how busy you are, there are some things that manage to work their way into your crowded schedule. As you think about "first things first," make God's Word a priority.

Heavenly Father, I love reading Your Word. Give my brain a boost today and help me memorize Your Word. I want to have it with me...and always available. Amen.

Taste and See

One of my favorite books of the Bible is 2 Timothy. It's short but passionate! This letter from the apostle Paul is a straightforward, heart-to-heart, hard-line call to Timothy to live a tough-as-nails, disciplined life. Why? So Timothy could glorify God with his life. You and I want that too, don't we? It's the only way we can successfully stand up to the trials of life. Everything God wants to say to you is in your Bible—from God's heart to yours. Scripture is God-breathed and inspired by Him (2 Timothy 3:16). In Psalm 34:8 you're invited to "taste and see that the LORD is good." Now that's an invitation you can't turn down! Relish and honor the counsel of the Lord.

Father, thank You for making sure I have access to Your wisdom and guidance. Open my eyes and heart so I can discern Your wisdom. Amen.

Press On

"I've lost the same pounds 15 times. I know I can do it again. Please pass the fries!" Sound familiar? As people who follow Christ, our lives shouldn't be about false starts, fad diets, and flashes of discipline. Maybe it's because I was an English teacher, but I pay careful attention to verbs—those wonderful action words. Verbs like *strive, reach, press, endure, run* are liberally sprinkled throughout the New Testament. And all of them are in verses pointing to the management of our life in Christ. Christian living is not a sprint or a spurt. Quite the opposite. The Bible encourages us to embrace life management as a marathon. Our dedication and service to God are to be characterized by a long, sustained, steady pace of pressing upward and onward toward becoming more like Christ and reaching out with His saving gospel.

Father, make sure there are refreshment stations along my path so I can be renewed and revived in Your love. I want to stay strong and steady as I serve and honor You. Amen.

Growing Your Marriage

Growing a Christian marriage and nurturing a life-long friendship takes work—sometimes hard work. It takes commitment, determination, time, and sacrifice. Next to your relationship with God, your marriage is your most urgent and most demanding endeavor.

If you're married, go above and beyond the call when it comes to managing your marriage. That's right. I said "managing your marriage." We are to help our husbands. Ephesians 5:22 says we're to follow our husband's leadership, to submit to him. What else are we called to do? To respect our husbands. And to love them. I can't think of any better relationship goals than these! Of your husband, I want you to be able to say wholeheartedly with enthusiasm, "This is my beloved, and this is my friend" (Song of Solomon 5:16).

Father, give me an attitude of graciousness and serv-anthood in my relationship with my husband. Help me overlook petty annoyances and concentrate on the positives of being married to him. Amen.

Nurture Your Marriage

Remember how much fun you had when you and your husband were dating? And when you were first married? I'm sure you did many spontaneous and slightly crazy things that brought out your love and laughter. For too many women, a lot of less important activities have replaced those special times. What would happen if you put much of that time, effort, and energy back into loving your husband?

The world wants to cloud your view of how important marriage is...and what it means to be married. Keep God's perspective in front of you at all times. Don't let anyone sell you on the idea that anything—apart from the Lord—is more important than actively nurturing your relationship with your husband. God wants your life and marriage to be filled with passion and purpose.

Heavenly Father, guard my marriage. Protect and grow the love I have for my husband...and the love he has for me. Watch over us and bless us. Amen.

Build Your House

Proverbs 14:1 says, "The wise woman builds her house." And that means wherever it is and no matter its size. Whether your place is a grand showcase home, an apartment, or a tent—keep it neat and tidy. Spend your energy building and bettering your home. Make it a place where God is honored and glorified. Create a safe haven for your family. When a home is built with wisdom, the rooms are filled with precious and pleasant riches (Proverbs 24:4). And don't forget attitude! Own the tasks before you. Tackle them with enthusiasm. Welcome the labor it takes to make a lovely home. It's our assignment. Take it on willingly, with passion and purpose.

Father, my home is a place of rest and safety for me and my family. Bless it with Your love. Remind me from time to time that the love we have and the security we feel at home is really rooted in You. Amen.

Just Enough

Whenever I speak on contentment, I share a special prayer. The ingredients call for "enough": Health enough to make work a pleasure. Wealth enough to support my needs. Strength enough to battle with difficulties. Grace enough to confess my sins and overcome them. Patience enough to keep at it until some good is accomplished. Charity enough to see some good in my neighbor. Love enough to be useful and helpful to others. Faith enough to make real the things of God. And hope enough to remove all anxious fears concerning the future.

Contentment is not based on present circumstances. Contentment is based on the person of God. He's all you need!

Jesus, You provide for my needs. Keep my mind on my priorities and guard my heart against wanting more than I need. Give me a generous spirit so I can share what You've given me with others. Amen.

Go on a Fast

I have a suggestion for you: Go on a fast. No, I'm not talking about food. I mean stop all unnecessary spending. And this idea isn't just for those with financial problems. Determine to go a month without frivolous purchases. A financial fast will do wonders for you. I know one woman who saved enough for a vacation just by cutting back on her stops for special coffee each morning. Besides this obvious benefit, being financially prudent will be like taking a deep breath of fresh air. It's cleansing! You'll acquire a renewed appreciation of all God is faithfully blessing you with. And you'll discover new strength for facing and dealing with other parts of your life. You'll never be wholly committed to God until your money is dedicated to Him.

Finances can be touchy, Lord. There are so many gadgets and clothes and things to buy. But You are my top priority. And reaching out financially to others in Your name is high on my "to do" list. My resources are Yours. Show me how You want me to use them. Amen.

Ministry Partners

"It sounds interesting. But I'm just not a committee person. It takes too much time, and I'm busy enough already." Sound familiar? I can't tell you the number of times women have said the same thing to me. And then there are the times I've said it to others. But trust me—serving is a blessing! When you and someone else minister together, a deep-level friendship is often born. You might be serving on a committee, setting up an event, or whatever, and a firm bond is established. What a blessing! Friendships based on service to God, on prayer together, on the study of God's Word are oh so rewarding. Once you've tasted a friendship formed with a ministry partner you'll want that element in all your friendships. As well you should. Soul partners and ministry partners. It's one of the best aspects of serving God!

Jesus, open my eyes to people around me. Guide me to someone I can relate to and be honest with. Use our friendship to meet our needs…and help others. Friends are a delightful side-effect of ministry. Amen.

Think on These Things

God has requirements for your thought life. Check out Philippians 4:8—"Whatever things are true... noble...just...pure...meditate on these things." So when you hear some "news" or come across information, ask yourself these important questions: Is it true? Is it just a rumor or suspicion? Would sharing it be noble? Would it reflect my Christian principles? Is it shoddy, cheap, beneath my dignity as a woman of God? Consider again the words *true, noble, just, pure, lovely, good, virtuous,* and *praiseworthy.* Say them out loud. Let their goodness roll through your mind and soul. Whatever you come across, choose to think on the things that speak the best of you, of God, and of others.

Father, keep my heart and mind pure. I want my thoughts to please You, and I want the words they provoke to encourage, build up, and show Your love to others. Amen.

Chocolate Chip Cookie Love

There's nothing that thrills my mother's heart more than two or three little ones sharing chocolate chip cookies at my house. As humans we have so little control over most of the events of our lives, but we do have a measure of say in establishing the atmosphere of our homes. And that includes filling the house with the wonderful aroma of chocolate chip cookies baking in the oven...just waiting for little hands to grab. What is under your roof reflects your love for your family and friends. Cherish and manage it as a place to love your family. If you're feeling overwhelmed by housework and upkeep—take heart. Creating a home is done one step at a time, one day at a time— one cookie at a time! Begin today.

Father, I so enjoy creating happy moments for my children and their friends. Show me how I can make my house even more comfortable so people will feel welcome and safe the moment they step in the door. Amen.

A Heart of Prayer

I remember my tenth spiritual anniversary so clearly. Resting before God, I was rejoicing in a decade of being His child. Overwhelmed with gratitude, I lifted my heart and prayed, "Lord, what do You see missing from my Christian life?" God responded immediately by focusing my mind on my prayer life. That spiritual birthday I reached for a book of blank pages that had been a gift and wrote: "I purpose to spend the next ten years developing a meaningful prayer life." I was surprised by the blessings that blossomed in my heart. The hymn by Johnson Oatman Jr. says, "Count your blessings, name them one by one, and it will surprise you what the Lord hath done." Such sweet music for the soul!

Father, today I praise You. Hear my voice and heart as I raise them up to You in worship and thanksgiving. You are so merciful...gracious...giving. I'm in awe of what You've done and how You willingly get involved in my life. Amen.

Consult God's Word

"I just don't know what to do. What if I make the wrong choice?" We all ask this question at times. How can we know God's will? Make the right decision? Truly our first thought should be, *What does God's Word say about this situation, this choice?* Always consult God's Word. Acts 17:10-11 says the Christians in Berea searched the Scriptures daily to find out the truth. Also, remember to pray about your situation. And how much do you pray? However much it takes to know God's will! Don't rush. Very few situations call for on-the-spot decision making. Consult God's Word and wait on Him in prayer. Psalm 33:11 says, "The counsel of the LORD stands forever, the plans of His heart to all generations."

Heavenly Father, how wonderfully You've taken care of my needs. You've given me Your Word to study and made Yourself available to me through prayer. You are amazing! Amen.

Friendships Take Time

"I've been at that church for nearly a year, and I still don't know one person I'd call a friend." That's so sad. We all need friends…casual friends, close friends, best friends. On any given day, many people cross your path. Don't be afraid to reach out, to include them in your activities. Think of them as friends sent by God. Consider them part of the purpose for your day. Perhaps they need a smile of encouragement. For others, a touch, a hug, or a kind word will draw them in. Maybe you can call someone to offer a cheerful greeting. As you manage your time and your life— all your projects and priorities—build in time for people…for their sakes and for yours. Be a friend to all…and cultivate several close friends as well.

Jesus, thank You for the people You've brought into my life. Help me give graciously when they need support. Let me encourage them with Your love and wisdom. If You know someone who needs a friend, send her my way! Amen.

Cry Out to God

Do you know people who don't like you? Has anyone ever said anything negative about you or cut you off or left you out? Try reading through the psalms for comfort. You'll be amazed by how much of the poetry centers on David's bouts with his enemies. He moans to God, wondering how long they will ruin his reputation (Psalm 4:2).

Enemies seem to be a fact of life, but we're not to hate them or fear them or even fight them. We're to cry out to God. Then we're to pray for our enemies... and pray about them. The good news is your foes will never achieve victory. God is watching over you (Numbers 14:9). And He promises to avenge you if needed (Deuteronomy 32:35). No one can frustrate God's plan or His promised protection and victory for your life.

Dear Jesus, it surprises and hurts me when I find out someone doesn't like me. Please open a path of communication so we can resolve any problems. And if that doesn't happen, thank You for watching over me. Amen.

A Gentle and Quiet Spirit

When I suggest the concept of a gentle and quiet spirit, I'm often met with the words, "You've got to be kidding! I can't be like that!" That would be true... except you have God's two great enablers—grace and peace—to help you. God has graced you with these gifts, giving you the assurance that you can live like this. Psalm 34:8 says, "Oh, taste and see that the LORD is good; blessed is the [woman] who trusts in Him." As you "put on" God's gentle and quiet spirit, as you rely on Him instead of your own efforts and emotions, you'll experience the goodness of the Lord.

Jesus, You want me to have a gentle and quiet spirit in the midst of the chaos that surrounds me? Okay. I'm sitting down with You now. Open my heart and flood me with Your peace. Amen.

Suffering

Suffering is a sad fact of life on earth. I so wish it weren't true. Jesus said, "In the world you will have tribulation" (John 16:33). But isn't it wonderful that He went on to add that we should "be of good cheer" because He has "overcome the world"? You can even experience great joy in your trials by looking forward to experiencing great glory with Jesus. I'm not making light of suffering. It's painful and hard. But by God's grace you can look to the Lord. He knows what it's like to suffer, "for we do not have a High Priest who cannot sympathize with our weaknesses, but was in all points tempted as we are, yet without sin" (Hebrews 4:15-16). So turn to Jesus today. Receive His love. Accept His comfort. Experience His glory.

Lord Jesus, life is such an interesting mix of joy and sorrow, pleasure and pain. When the suffering comes, remind me that You are my strength and deliverer. Amen.

A Heart of Humility

Are you praying about a situation…but God doesn't seem to be doing anything about it? Be assured that God is always at work! He's directing the course of events to bring about His perfect will…in His perfect time. That's the difficult part, isn't it? God's timing! I can't say it too often: Read your Bible regularly! God's Word will help you understand His will for your life. Pray regularly. Prayer helps you bring your will in line with God's will. Worship regularly. Times of quiet before God allow Him to teach you. And serve others regularly. Your family first…and then everyone who crosses your path. These "regular" events in your life will keep you depending upon God and trusting His will for your life. Humbly come before Him, knowing He is the one and only God and that He loves you.

Father, You are an awesome God who watches over everything. Nothing happens that You don't know about. I will patiently wait on You for the answers to my prayers. I trust You. Amen.

The Lord Will Provide

Do you know that one of God's names is Yahweh-jireh? It means "the LORD will provide" (Genesis 22:14). That's a powerful promise and one you can count on every day, all the time. When you feel overwhelmed by something you've been asked to do or something's taking place in your life and you just can't see how you can handle it, remember—and believe— "the LORD will provide." You might have to replace your common sense and reason with faith in Him, but stick with the Lord's promise. Faith will bloom. The "seen" is replaced with the "unseen." Name your greatest challenge and then take a step of obedience and faith to see the gracious blessings of God. "The LORD will provide!"

Lord Jesus, I need You to provide for me in so many ways. Thank You in advance for always watching over me and my family and for meeting all our needs. Amen.

Love Is Important to God

You can't read very far in the Bible before realizing that love is very important to God. To love one another—our husbands, our children, our neighbors, even our enemies—is commanded in God's Word (Matthew 5:44; John 13:34). When God sent His Son, Jesus Christ, as an offering for our sin, the model for love was set forever. It doesn't get much clearer than John 15:12, "This is My commandment, that you love one another as I have loved you." His love gave, served, and died for us. Will you ask God to fill you with that kind of love? The love modeled by our Savior? Be prepared for an amazing transformation!

Lord Jesus, You gave us the perfect example of love. I trust that as You continue to transform me into Your image, You will help me show Your love to the people around me. Amen.

Learning to Adapt

"I feel totally unappreciated. It's easy to say, 'Serve your husband,' but what about his part?" I hear this from wives all the time...and I've heard it from my own heart as well. So what do you do? Although out of step with the world's view, God tells us to treat our husbands as if Jesus were standing before us. Is that a little hard to swallow? Ephesians 5:22 says, "Wives, be subject [or learn to adapt] to your own husbands, as to the Lord." God is calling us to a love and service that's not self-seeking. Our intent is to love as Jesus loved... and to pray for others—including our husbands!—to respond to God's message of love through us.

Lord Jesus, a lot of things were wrong in my life, and You died for me anyway. May I follow Your example and love my husband even though he's not always perfect or receptive. Amen.

In Everything Give Thanks

When life is good it's easy for praise and thanksgiving to flow from our lips. But when life gets tough, that's an entirely different story. Yet the Bible says, "In everything give thanks" (1 Thessalonians 5:18). Everything? I'm afraid so! Think of it this way: When you'd rather stay stuck in your depression but you choose to look beyond your pain to see or trust in the Lord's purpose, that's sacrificial praise.

So often it's out of the darkness of my trials that I find God's joy magnified in my life. Think of a beautiful diamond displayed against a black background. The dark makes the stone shine all the more. What a great picture of what Christ has done for us.

Jesus, whenever I focus on my problems, help me see them as opportunities for You to do amazing things. And thank You for using every situation to make me more like You. Amen.

Someone to Pull You Up

I've discovered there are three kinds of acquaintances in life. The ones who pull you down. Those who pull you along. And those who pull you up. The kind of friend you want is the one who pulls you along spiritually. A gal that's moving toward the same zeal in Christ you are. Even better is a friend who pulls you up! One that's a step (or two!) ahead of you. Someone who inspires you and is willing to mentor you to greater growth. Ask God for that kind of accountability in your life. Then do your part to be that kind of friend to her and to others. Sharing a daily passion for God's Word is an amazing bond!

Jesus, You have blessed me with such wonderful friends. Thank You for teaching me through them. Help me encourage them to seek You and trust You every day. Amen.

Friendship Gives

True friends don't keep score. Have you ever said, "We had the Smiths over for dinner. I wonder why they haven't invited us to their house?" Here's one that's even more sensitive: True friends don't go over the top when a birthday is forgotten. What are other attributes of true friends? They don't worry when a phone call isn't returned right away. They don't always have to sit together. They don't get upset if you spend time with someone else. They understand if you're part of other groups.

True friends rejoice with you. They honor you and appreciate you. Friendship gives and asks for no payment.

Are you a true friend?

Lord Jesus, I pray for Your grace to rest on me so I can love and support my friends without expecting to be repaid. Help me love sacrificially and experience the true joy of serving others just as You did. Amen.

God's Temple

"Hey, back off! It's my body and I can do with it what I please!" The only thing wrong with this statement is that it's totally wrong. As in incorrect. Mistaken. Not even close to being right. What's the truth? God owns your body. And He calls it a "temple." Read it for yourself in 1 Corinthians 6:19. And He has a few rules you should follow. Flee sexual immorality (1 Corinthians 6:18). First John 2:15 says, "Do not love the world or the things in the world." Stay away from every form of evil (Proverbs 4:14). The wonderful thing is that your body, soul, and spirit have been "bought" by Jesus Christ when He suffered on the cross for your sins. Keep your body holy!

Lord Jesus, please help me remember that my body was created by You, and that I am merely a steward of it. I choose this day to care for my body with healthful food, sleep, rest, and exercise. Amen.

Just Say No

Say no. Try it: No. The next time you want more of some tempting food, say no. When you want to turn off the alarm and go back to sleep, say no. If you're working along on an important project and a friend calls and says, "Hey, let's get together for lunch." What do you say? No. To live out God's plan for your life requires saying no now and then. In Matthew 16:24, Jesus doesn't say, "Fulfill yourself." He says, "Deny yourself." You're called to discipline yourself—your body, your time, your spirit. Scripture calls this life a race...so get into the race. Run the race. Stay on course and run to win!

Lord, I want to say yes to You and to those things You call me to. Thank You for grace when I don't say no as I should, and for opportunities to redeem those moments when I focused only on what I wanted. Amen.

Priming the Prayer Pump

"I'd pray more, but, frankly, I'm not exactly sure how to go about it." I used to say that. If you could see my study, you'd notice immediately there's an entire shelf of books on prayer. I read them because they teach me how to pray.

I especially love the book *The Prayers of Susanna Wesley*. She had such a passion for God and for prayer. If there was ever an ideal of a woman after God's own heart it was Susanna Wesley. And talk about busy! She had 19 children. (Oops—there goes that excuse!) I sometimes prime my prayer pump by praying one of her uplifting prayers. Somehow her heartfelt outpouring warms my heart and loosens my tongue…and Susanna's passion for prayer becomes my own.

Jesus, taking time to talk with You is one of my favorite things to do. But I often allow other duties and commitments to keep me from a regular prayer time. I purpose to make talking with You my top priority. Then there will be time for everything else. Amen.

Simplify Your Life

Is it time to simplify your life? One management expert said a routine "makes unskilled people capable of doing what it took a genius to do before." It's amazing what the simple discipline of keeping a schedule will help you accomplish. Take a careful look at the life of Jesus. He never seemed to be in a hurry. He was never rushed and never breathless. He was unhurried because His schedule was based on God's priorities for His life. John 5:36 says, "The works which the Father has given Me to finish—the very works that I do—bear witness of Me, that the Father has sent Me." Look at your life closely, write down a plan, and follow through.

Lord, I long to honor You with each hour of my day. I choose to give my time to You. This is another area of stewardship, and I want to be a good steward. I pray for wisdom as I plan each hour of every day. Amen.

Pray for Your Husband

Matthew 6:21 says, "Where your treasure is, there your heart will be also." One of the best things you can do to improve your marriage is to be a woman of prayer for your husband. You'll find an amazing thing happens as you spend your precious time praying for your husband and your marriage. Your commitment to your union will be more refreshed and reenergized than any number of date nights could ever accomplish. When the "treasure" of your time and effort is spent in prayer, your heart becomes consumed with the object of your devotion—your husband in this case. Prayer will do wonders for you and your spouse.

Jesus, watch over my husband. Be with him in moments of stress and worry. Comfort him when he is anxious about any area of his life. Help me be sensitive to his needs and be a blessing to him all the years of our life together. Amen.

Being the Right Person

Marriage is so much more than finding the right person. You also need to be the right person. Genesis 2:18 says your role is to be your husband's helper. I realize that's not a popular message in today's culture, but it's what God says. A woman whose example is Jesus follows His lead and serves. Yes, it's nice if your spouse helps you, but don't get caught up in expecting it or, worse, resenting it if it doesn't happen. Being a servant to your husband is not about your being less than him. It's all about being more...more like Jesus. Go ahead and test the water. Trust the Lord. Make that man of yours the most important person in your life.

Lord, I pray my husband will know how much I love him, not only by my words but also by my deeds. I want to be his helper and cheerleader and lover. I want to be his confidante in every area of his life. Amen.

A Strong Faith

Do you work in a non-Christian environment? Have you heard coworkers and friends say Christians are right-wing radicals? If you haven't spoken up, maybe today needs to be the day. But where do you get the strength to do that? Two keys are strong faith and trust in God. Christians who contend for the faith must be reading God's Word regularly. They must be well-grounded in God's truth to protect their own faith and answer reasonable questions nonbelievers might ask.

Don't hesitate to ask God for His guidance in your situation. For inspiration and how-tos, read biographies of courageous believers who stood up for God. Get prayer support. And when you do speak, do it gently. Say your piece and let others talk. Don't get into arguing matches (2 Timothy 2:24-26). God will bless your words and use them…if not at that moment, definitely later.

Father, please give me Your gracious, straightforward manner when I hear people put down Christians. Allow me to speak the truth in love…and leave the convicting and convincing to You. Amen.

Life's Most Difficult Assignment

Changing diapers, cleaning spills, staying up all night with a sick child. This isn't exactly what we think of when we think of being godly. But hang in there! Your rewards for taking care of even the most mundane chores are great. Your godly mothering impacts all eternity! Raising your children is life's most difficult assignment, but it's also the most rewarding. I've been a mother for more than 40 years, and now I'm the grandmother of 8 beautiful grandkids. What a privilege and joy these wonderful human beings bring into my life. But I must say that I am happy to have those "diaper and spill" days over! I encourage you to give mothering all the passion and purpose it deserves. No journey could be more of an adventure, and no road is more honorable.

Jesus, thank You for the privilege of being a mother. Help me never take this precious role for granted. Some days I become weary, but You renew my soul so I can continue to give to the little ones in my life. Amen.

Managing a Home

Do you know that managing your home is a spiritual issue? Yes, you read correctly. I love what author Elisabeth Elliot said: "A sloppy life speaks of a sloppy faith." We're careful in our faith…careful to tend to our spiritual growth, careful to obey God's Word, and careful to maintain the spiritual disciplines of prayer, worship, and giving. So why shouldn't we also be careful of how we manage our homes? Titus 2:5 says we are to be homemakers. That's not a put-down. Far from it! Creating a safe and comfortable place for your husband, children, and you is a privilege and a significant accomplishment.

Lord, I recognize my unique place in our home. I am responsible for much of the beauty, joy, and peace my family experiences. Thank You for giving me a family to love and a home to care for. Help me diligently love and care for them to the best of my abilities. Amen.

God Meets All Your Needs

Dear friend, are you worried? Do you wonder where the money to pay the rent or mortgage is coming from, whether you'll have enough food, how you're going to pay your bills? If that's you today, I know exactly how it feels. It's scary. The next time you're tempted to think God isn't meeting all your needs…or isn't meeting them very well, remember: He is whether it looks and feels like it or not. Engage your faith. Faith is defined in Hebrews 11:1 as "the substance of things hoped for, the evidence of things not seen." As a woman of God, your faith can be lived out in your confident assurance that God is in control. Do you believe God will provide for all your needs? And the answer? Absolutely!

Lord, I choose to be a woman of faith. You have never forsaken me. You've never left me on my own. You are entirely trustworthy, and I praise You for providing everything I truly need. Amen.

Addicted to Shopping

Do you love to shop? Is buying things too high on your priority list? Here's a new thought for you: Pray instead of spending. I'm not kidding. Create a list of the items you think you need. Look at the list often and add to it when necessary. Then pray over each item every day. Pray for the patience to wait for God to meet your real needs. Ask God to help you discern if you should purchase a particular item. By doing this you'll be blessed in three specific ways:

You'll enjoy victory over temptation.

You'll hold back on further debt.

Best of all, God is glorified when you trust Him for your needs.

Take Proverbs 22:7 to heart: "The borrower is servant to the lender." This makes sense to me.

Lord, praying about things instead of buying them seems like a great idea. I can see how it could change my life. I promise to start today. Help me be faithful in this. Amen.

Your Best Friend

Wouldn't life be so much simpler if there weren't so many people? We all have to manage our lives so that God's priorities are at the top of the list. If you're married, your spouse is to be your greatest concern (after God, of course). He's to be the largest investment of your time and energy. Titus 2:4 says to love your husband as your best friend, a cherished brother in Christ, an intimate mate. If that's not what you're experiencing, ask God to work first in your heart. Ask Him to help you want to be your husband's companion and friend. Then rearrange your life so there's more time for him. Rekindle your friendship. You'll be glad you did.

Lord, I don't always think of my husband as my best friend. I remember days when we were closer than we are now. I long for those and see that I'll need to change my priorities for that to happen again. I trust You to provide the encouragement I'll need along the way. Amen.

Your Driving Force

Next to God, the heartbeat of your life as a wife and mother centers on your husband, your children, and your grandchildren. What will be the long-term results of your life? When I die I don't want to leave a legacy of club memberships, girlfriend outings, or even successful business ventures. I want to leave behind people I've influenced for the Lord. I want them to have a deep, lasting love for God, strong relationships with family and friends, great character, and the knowledge they are loved.

What do you want to leave? First Corinthians 13:8 says, "Love never fails." Love suffers long and is kind, it bears all things, hopes all things, endures all things (verses 4-7). Make this kind of love your driving force. Amazing things will happen!

Lord, it all comes back to priorities. Some of mine are good. I think You're pleased with them. But a lot of them could be better. Help me choose the best over the good and see the amazing things You want to do through me. Amen.

Loving Your In-Laws

"Honor your father and your mother" (Exodus 20:12). Does that include your in-laws? What if your mother-in-law is pushy, judgmental, and difficult? And what if your father-in-law puts you down all the time? Well, the full version of Exodus 20:12 says, "Honor your father and your mother, that your days may be long upon the land which the LORD your God is giving you." Pretty serious stuff, wouldn't you say?

As a woman of God, you must nurture your relationship with your parents. And if you're married, the same attention needs to be given to your husband's parents. Building solid, loving relationships with them isn't optional. I encourage you to have a positive attitude...even when it's hard. Trust God for the grace and love and resources you need to get along with everyone—including your parents and in-laws.

Lord, I believe You have a blessing for me if I honor my parents and my husband's parents. Help me keep my temper under control and not let little hurts grow into bitterness. I want to love them as You do. Amen.

A Kind Word

We all have "chance" meetings...but you and I both know there's really no such thing. God arranges these encounters. When they occur we may only have a few seconds to determine what to do or say. Be prepared! Have ready words of encouragement and appreciation. When you run into someone, ask yourself, "What can I give this person? A word of encouragement? A listening ear? A comforting touch? A big smile and an enthusiastic hello?"

People are all around us—family, friends, and strangers. Who knows what's going on in their lives. Who knows the sadness, the hardship, the heartaches, the trials. Do you ever consider your words and actions in these brief encounters as ministry? God may use you to give people the only kind words they'll receive today...or the only gentle hugs.

Lord, You've given me so much. Help me embrace every person I meet today, whether it is with an actual hug or simply with kind eyes or a gentle word. Let me be generous with Your love. Amen.

The Little Details

Friendships are wonderful things, aren't they? And it's often the little details that make a huge difference. I so enjoy it when someone lets me know she's praying for me. One friend sent me "a prayer angel," a little kneeling angel for my desk. Each day when I look at it I'm reminded that she is praying for me. Now that's a loving friend! One note I received included a quote from Hebrews 6:10 NLT: "God is not unfair. He will not forget how hard you have worked for him and how you have shown your love to him by caring for other Christians"…like me, she added.

Be that special friend in someone's life. Who can you encourage today?

Jesus, what a privilege to encourage others. Help me think of someone today who would be especially blessed by hearing from me. Give me words to say to meet her exactly at her point of need. Amen.

Making Wise Decisions

Not a second goes by that you and I aren't making decisions. As you listen to someone speak—and the operative word is *listen*—you need to carefully decide how to answer. And when there's a crisis and you have to make a quick decision, be as careful as you can. I have an idea! When there are unexpected quiet moments in that whirlwind life of yours, put that time to good use. Consider your priorities and values. Evaluate whether they're right on or if they need some adjusting. When you have a good handle on what you believe and why, making decisions becomes easier and there's less potential for making big mistakes.

God, uncover my motives today. Help me dig down to my real beliefs—the ones I act out in daily life. I want to let You conform those beliefs to Your desires. Amen.

In Tough Times...

It's hard to be grateful when everything is going wrong. And we've all experienced that. But gratitude in all situations is an incredible quality within our reach because we love God. Be encouraged during difficult times. God knows your joys and sorrows. And He knows your strengths and your weaknesses, your husband's too, and your children's needs. He's aware of all the challenges you face. He knows your pain if you've just lost your job. If you're single with the desire to be married. If your in-laws are giving you fits. God doesn't overlook anything. Nothing escapes Him. He, in His wisdom, is always working toward His perfect goals for your life. And He acts with flawless precision. Now that's something to be thankful for, dear friend!

In this confusion and difficulty, God, it's easy to forget that You're here and You care. I know You have control of all things. Now, Lord, help me make that knowledge real in my life today. Amen.

Be Purposeful

"Plan my day? With my husband and kids' input and crazy schedules? You've got to be kidding!" Like it or not we have to choose what to do and what not to do. I have a friend who always crams in one more project, one more event, one more errand. She's always late and always frazzled. Setting priorities will make your day and your life go so much more smoothly.

So plan your life according to God's priorities. Schedule your day so God is glorified and the people in your life are blessed. There's beauty—and sanity!—in organizing. It takes time and effort, but it's worth it. And although you make your plans, God sometimes has something different in mind...so be flexible and go with "Plan B" when necessary.

Father, I confess my pride in neglecting to plan. Some days I think I can do it all! Or I've tried to control everything and it's fallen apart, but I don't want to admit it to You. Today I want my life to reflect Your order and beauty. Amen.

You're Gifted by God

Has someone asked you to do something you've never done before? Maybe you've been asked to lead a Bible study, volunteer at a local nonprofit, or host a retreat? Say yes! You're more gifted than you think. I'm encouraging you and challenging you to take a chance and do something different. Use the gifts God has given you. First Peter 4:10 says, "Each of you should use whatever gift you have received to serve others, as faithful stewards of God's grace in its various forms" (NIV). There was a time when I had to step out and take on the risk of something new to meet the call of God on my life. As He revealed my gifts and how to use them, He gave me the strength and grace for the ministry I have today. What gifts has God given you? Use them for Him!

God, thank You for granting me gifts that allow me to serve You and reach out to others. I offer myself to You today, to help me grow in You so You can use me. Amen.

Your Spiritual Gift

A lot of women ask, "Do I have a spiritual gift?" My answer? First Corinthians 12 says,

> There are diversities of gifts...The manifestation of the Spirit is given to each one for the profit of all: for to one is given the word of wisdom through the Spirit, to another the word of knowledge through the same Spirit, to another faith by the same Spirit (verses 4,7-9).

Yes, you have a spiritual gift! What do you enjoy doing for others? The activity or process of your gift brings joy. Another attribute of a spiritual gift is your service will bless people and you. Your gift will also create opportunities for repeat service. Giftedness doesn't end, although it may modify as time goes on.

I want to take an honest look at myself, Father. Help me see what I'm already doing with Your Spirit's gift to me. Please give me confidence to identify and move forward in that gift. Amen.

Be a Cheerleader

Some of the "worst" words in the Bible, in my opinion, are Paul's admonishment to the leadership at the church in Philippi. He said, "Help these women" (Philippians 4:3)! Neither one of the two women Paul refers to was an example of Christian maturity. They were causing enough trouble that Paul stepped in and asked the church leaders to take charge and get them to settle their differences.

Friends, it takes time, sacrifice, preparation, and courage to be involved in any ministry. So let's be encouragers...let's come alongside the people who serve. In fact, let's be even more radical and volunteer to help them!

Father, You've given me so much! Today help me live in gratitude to You and move out and give to others. May I remind them how great You are, how You provide everything we need, and how much You delight in us. Amen.

Cooking and Cleaning

There's nothing you can do that God can't use. From cleaning up to being a keynote speaker at a retreat, you can contribute to and be part of the work of Christ. What can we do when we set our minds to it? Luke 8:1-3 describes a group of faithful women who used their money and means to support Jesus and His disciples on their preaching tours. Martha and Mary were two sisters who regularly hosted Jesus and His disciples for dinner and rest in their home (Luke 10:38). The mother of John Mark hosted a prayer meeting at her house (Acts 12:12). In Romans 16:1-2 Phoebe is described as a servant in her church and a helper of many. What a thrilling parade of women! And what did they do? Cooking, cleaning, working, praying, hosting, giving, helping. Nothing you and I can't do!

Lord, may I never underestimate the gifts You've given me. Help me see how I can offer practical, hands-on help when needed. Thank You for the opportunity to be a modern-day Phoebe—a helper of many. Amen.

Watch, Listen, Act

There's no better time than the present to notice other people's needs and do something about them. Yes, even during your busiest times. Proverbs 20:12 says, "The hearing ear and the seeing eye, the Lord has made them both." Be watching and listening to those around you. That's exactly what God does in our lives. He watches and listens and responds in loving care for our every need. Follow Dorcas's example. She was a woman "full of good works and charitable deeds which she did" (Acts 9:36). This thoughtful lady noticed the widows needed clothes, and so she acted on it and made some for them. Ask God to lead you to people who need encouragement, support, and prayer. Notice those around you and keep a keen eye out for ways you can actively help.

Jesus, surely You set up divine appointments every day so I can be used by You to meet a need. Help me watch and listen for those opportunities to say a kind word or do a charitable deed. May others see Your goodness in my outstretched hands. Amen.

The Things of God

Redeeming your time is so important. What do I mean? Time is redeemed when you make the most of your life by fulfilling God's purposes. As you line up your life and seize every opportunity for useful service, your life takes on an efficient quality. That may be difficult to imagine since you're so busy, but as you focus on doing the business of God, time expands. I don't know who wrote this poem, but it's so true:

> I have only just a minute.
> Only sixty seconds in it...
> Just a tiny little minute.
> But eternity is in it.

As your heart becomes more dedicated to God, you'll reclaim, recover, retrieve, rescue, and regain the minutes, hours, and days of your life for His glory.

Jesus, what a precious gift time is! Please keep me aware of my stewardship of this great award. Help me make good use of every hour, realizing that once spent, it can never be returned to me. Amen.

A "Today" Resolution

You don't have to wait until New Year's Day to make a resolution about your schedule. Why not make one today? First, pray over your priorities: "Lord, what is Your will for me at this time of my life?" Now plan through your priorities and prepare a schedule: "Lord, when should I do the things that live out these priorities today?" Ask the Lord to give you direction for your day: "Lord, I only have a limited amount of time left in my day. What do I need to focus on?" Prepare for tomorrow: "Lord, how can I better live out Your plan for my life?" Let the Lord know you appreciate Him: "Lord, thank You for this day...and the opportunity to talk with You directly." Then go forth with confidence and joy.

Lord, my life is Yours. I want to please You in everything I do. I need Your guidance and strength and stamina. I love You. Amen.

A Special Time

Why not plan a special night for your family? If you're not married, get friends together. Give everyone plenty of notice, especially if teens are involved. When the time comes around, prepare a festive meal, go out to dinner, or order pizza!

Later, gather around and have everyone share what they've done in the past three months that was fun and meaningful. Encourage each person to share a goal or dream…and be supportive. Dreams aren't always based on current reality. Talk about the childhood antics of the kids, how you and your husband grew up, what your parents did, where your grandparents lived. Share your faith experiences…and let others share theirs. End your time together by drawing people's names out of a hat and committing to doing two nice things for that person during the week.

Lord, You've given me a wonderful family and awesome friends. I delight in being with these people You've given me to cherish…and I especially delight in You. Amen.

Love Is a Decision

Loving your husband is a daily choice. Love may start out as a good feeling, but to love someone long-term is an act of the will. It means loving someone even when he may not be lovable at that particular moment. Hopefully your husband is your best friend. Enjoy being with him. Spoil him. Think about him. Pray for him. Encourage him.

But what if you don't feel this way? The question remains, "Will you love your husband?" Do everything you can—starting right now—to restore your love. Pray for him. Do little acts of kindness for him. Express your love in every way you can. Thoughtful deeds and kind thoughts will reenergize your love and revitalize your marriage. Love is blossoming in you, my friend.

Lord, loving another person can sometimes be trying. But by Your grace I can love my spouse completely. I choose to honor and serve this man I call husband. Help me be the wife he needs. Work in his life so he will be all You envisioned. Amen.

The Hardest Work

Raising kids can be an uphill battle. I know that from experience! Although we love them dearly, they aren't always the little angels we wish they'd be. When we don't feel very loving does that mean we're being bad mothers? No! We're human...and God knows that. A godly mother loves God with all her heart, soul, mind, and strength. And she passionately and consistently teaches her children to do the same. No one has more potential for godly influence on your children than you and your husband. Pray every day for these little ones and pour God's Word into their lives. Ask God to give you wisdom as you show your kids you love them. Amid the joy of raising children will be some of the hardest life work you'll ever do. And it's one of God's highest callings. Hang in there!

Father, I need Your strength, grace, and mercy as I deal with my kids today. I want to shower them with unconditional love and support. And I want to open their minds and hearts to You. Amen.

Pray, My Friend

"I'd pray more often, but I run out of stuff to say." I can certainly relate. To grow in the Lord, the reading and studying of God's Word is essential. And so is prayer. In fact, prayer is one of the privileges we have as Christians.

The Bible calls us to a life of faithful prayer, which isn't always easy. One of the best incentives to pray is that it strengthens us and short-circuits our tendency to sin. Prayer also gives us the strength and wisdom to follow through on the teachings in the Bible.

If prayer is difficult for you, set aside a small amount of time for prayer every day. Gradually increase that time as you settle into this routine. And you can talk to God about anything. No question, no problem, no concern is too big or too small for Him to handle!

Lord, calm my spirit as I come to You with praise and share my concerns. Give me the courage to talk to You and the patience to listen for Your response. Amen.

Heaven on Earth

Would you describe what goes on in your home as "heaven on earth"? That's quite an expression, isn't it? Heaven on earth! Do you know that your home life is meant to be exactly that? The Bible uses home life and marriage as illustrations of God's relationship with His church, with the people who choose to follow Him. And when we live out our God-ordained roles and fulfill our God-given assignments, others take notice and see proof of our special relationship with the Lord.

You have the privilege of presenting a picture of what heaven will be like to those around you. When you pursue with passion and purpose God's design for a woman, a homemaker, a wife, a mother, you establish a home that reflects the order and beauty of life in heaven. An amazing opportunity, isn't it?

I'm only human, Lord. How can I have a home and marriage that reflects Your perfect love, Your perfect peace? I want to grow in these areas. I want to point people to You. Amen.

That One Thing

You may have heard the expression, "But one thing I do..." What is that "one thing" in your life? In Philippians 3:13-14 the apostle Paul said his "one thing" was to forget what is behind and reach forward to what's ahead, pressing on toward the goal to win the prize of the upward call of God in Christ Jesus. I encourage you to be like a runner—never looking back at the ground already covered, but, instead, moving forward deliberately. According to Paul's example, we should concentrate our energies on moving forward into the future.

Where are you putting your focus? Have your goal in view—and keep your eyes, your heart, and your life fixed on the end of the race. We conquer by continuing...so press on!

Father, thank You for forgiving me and taking care of my past...and my future! Help me look ahead to see how I can serve You and run the course You've set before me. Amen.

God's Peace and Joy

Do you struggle with depression? With negative thoughts? God promises you joy. No matter what your circumstances, you can have joy in Him. Philippians 4:4 says, "Rejoice in the Lord always. Again I will say, rejoice!" Rejoicing is not an option. And the truth is that the kind of rejoicing the Bible talks about often comes from a life of pain and hardship. But God's peace and joy will prevail. Philippians 4:6-7 says, "Be anxious for nothing, but in everything by prayer and supplication, with thanksgiving, let your requests be made known to God; and the peace of God, which surpasses all understanding, will guard your hearts and minds through Christ Jesus." God's peace stands guard against all those things that attack your mind and heart. Through prayer you'll also experience the joy God gives—His joy—in abundance (John 17:13-14).

Father, You are an awesome God! You not only give me the strength and fortitude I need to make it through my trials, but You also shower me with Your joy and peace along the way. Thank You! Amen.

Second Fiddle

An interviewer asked famed conductor Leonard Bernstein, "What's the most difficult instrument to play?" Good-naturedly he replied, "Second fiddle!" He added, "And if no one plays second, there's no harmony." We need to be more than willing to be God's servants. We need to revel in the opportunities He gives us to serve.

Do you have someone you work with, serve with shoulder to shoulder? A woman you help as she serves the Lord? The apostle Paul said of Timothy in Philippians 2, "But I trust in the Lord Jesus to send Timothy to you shortly...I have no one like-minded, who will sincerely care for your state" (verses 19-20). I pray that you'll spend time with a mentor in ministry and in prayer and Bible study. I encourage you to mature in your usefulness. Be content to play "second fiddle."

> *Jesus, You were so humble and willing to serve. I want to follow Your example. Keep me from being caught up in wanting to be in charge of everything. Help me look for places to serve and uplift others. Amen.*

Pray for Your Children

Praying for your children is the most powerful way you can care for them. Most times your heart will naturally overflow in prayer for them. And even when they're causing trouble or your patience is wearing thin, a quick prayer will calm your nerves and soothe your children. You'll be amazed at the huge difference prayer will make in the lives of your little ones. Ask God to show you how to let them know that after Him and your husband, they're more important than all the other people in your life.

Be ready to show your love. Set aside time each day to pray for your kiddos. And don't forget to pray for them when they're around. That lets them know you and God love them. It also helps them feel more secure and models prayer.

Praying for your kids is some of the best time you'll ever invest. Prayer is a powerful privilege!

Jesus, protect these little lives You've placed in my care. Help me be patient, calm, loving, and supportive. Open their hearts to You. Amen.

I Shall Not Want

When is your church's next retreat? How long until your Bible study group gets together for fellowship? Do you catch an occasional radio broadcast or do quick devotional readings once in a while? Too often we neglect nurturing our spiritual lives by getting by on quick fixes. If your desire is to grow spiritually, you'll need to spend quality time in God's Word and more time in prayer.

I love Psalm 23, which starts, "The LORD is my shepherd; I shall not want." This so reminds me of my need for Him. Are you following the Shepherd? "He makes me to lie down in green pastures; He leads me beside the still waters. He restores my soul; He leads me in the paths of righteousness for His name's sake" (verses 2 and 3). Are you lying down in green pastures as the verse says? Are you feeding to your heart's content on His provision?

Father, You are my Shepherd. I want to follow You all of my days on earth…and into eternity. Restore my soul and refresh my spirit today. Amen.

Where He Leads

What would you do if God suddenly called you to a different ministry? Sometime when you have a few minutes for yourself, take a card and write these words: *anything, anywhere, anytime, at any cost.* Then date the note. Can you in all honesty sign it? God's role is to lead us. Our job is to follow.

How are you doing? Have you looked into God's wonderful face and into His eyes of love and whispered, "Truly, dear Lord, where You lead me, I will follow"? Do these words express the deep longing of your heart? Are you following Him today? If not, will you?

God, You are my reason for living, my salvation, my comfort, my provider, my love. I choose today to follow You every step of the way. When the way gets hard and I falter, encourage me and give me strength. Amen.

A Model for the Home

The woman of Proverbs 31 is a great model for home management. She does her husband good. She makes household items for her family and to sell. She shops wisely. She's very industrious. She buys land, plants crops, and invests. She keeps herself fit. This woman helps the needy. She's honorable, wise, and kind. She looks forward to the future. And her children and husband sing her praises. And no wonder!

Look to this amazing woman for inspiration. With God's help, you too can accomplish much. He calls you to tend your home and serve your family, and you do that in so many ways. But are you doing the best you can do? I encourage you to master new skills, express your creativity, and find new ways to help. Even if you work outside your home, you can make your home even better than "home sweet home." What an awesome privilege!

Father, thank You for blessing me with a home and for family and friends that fill it. Help me be industrious and cheerful as I encourage and serve everyone who comes in. Amen.

Praise God!

I'm so glad you're God's friend, that you have the promise of His blessings in your life. In Psalm 16:11, David says of God, "You will show me the path of life; in Your presence is fullness of joy; at Your right hand are pleasures forevermore." God will never fail you or change His mind about you. In His loving care you have a shelter in the storm and a haven when life bats you around. In His loving care you can have a generous heart because He provides abundantly. Use Psalm 23:6 as an affirmation of what you know to be true: "Surely goodness and mercy shall follow me all the days of my life; and I will dwell in the house of the LORD forever." Praise His holy name!

Jesus, I praise You! You've given me many astounding gifts and provided for and watched over me in countless ways. You are so wonderful, so powerful, so mighty, and so everlasting. And You love me. Amazing. Amen.

A Positive Attitude

It may surprise you to know that a positive attitude and the giving of thanks is willful…a choice you make. Giving thanks is a conscious decision, and it's also commanded by God. His Word tells us to give thanks always and for all things, in everything and evermore. First Thessalonians 5:16-18 says, "Rejoice always, pray without ceasing, in everything give thanks; for this is the will of God in Christ Jesus for you." That's pretty clear!

And the decision to do just that—to give thanks… no matter what…in whatever situation—has a powerful effect on your attitude. Not only that, it also has a huge impact on everyone around you. Philippians 4:7 says the peace of God that surpasses all understanding is available to you and me. Now that's something to be thankful for!

Father, even though You've blessed me so much, I still get stuck on what's not going right and the trials I face. Gently remind me that You're always with me. I want to maintain a thankful heart toward You! Amen.

Good News!

Do you know Jesus? Is He your Lord and Savior? Romans 3:23 reveals that we all have sinned. We all fall short of God's glory. And the penalty for sin is death...spiritual death. The Good News is Christ died for you (and me)! Romans 10:9 says, "If you confess with your mouth the Lord Jesus and believe in your heart that God has raised Him from the dead, you will be saved." Please take this opportunity to give your life to Jesus. Open yourself to His love and truth. Ask Him to come into your heart and be with you forever. He's waiting for you!

And if you already know Jesus, praise His holy name!

Jesus, I yearn to experience Your love. In my sin-filled heart I don't even come close to being as You are. Thank You for coming to earth and paying the price for my sins so I can know You personally. I accept Your free gift of salvation. Help me grow in You every day. Amen.

God's Grace

Do you know that the sustaining power of God is packaged in His grace? Life can deliver some tough blows, but God's marvelous grace enables us to go from strength to strength through all the trials. Second Corinthians 12:9 promises that God's grace is sufficient—that it is made perfect in our weakness. I know that encourages my heart. Take that trial you're experiencing and bring it to the Lord. Lay it at His feet. Look to Him. Count on His grace and power in every situation. It's there. It's given to you. And it brings the peace you so long for.

Bless you in your journey to become a woman after God's own heart.

Father, my heart overflows with the love and blessings You've given me. Even in the midst of my trials and sorrow I can be joyful in my heart because I know You are in charge. Amen.

Books by Elizabeth George

- Beautiful in God's Eyes
- Beautiful in God's Eyes for Young Women
- Breaking the Worry Habit…Forever
- Finding God's Path Through Your Trials
- Following God with All Your Heart
- The Heart of a Woman Who Prays
- Life Management for Busy Women
- Loving God with All Your Mind
- Loving God with All Your Mind DVD and Workbook
- A Mom After God's Own Heart
- A Mom After God's Own Heart Devotional
- Moments of Grace for a Woman's Heart
- One-Minute Inspirations for Women
- Prayers to Calm Your Heart
- Quiet Confidence for a Woman's Heart
- Raising a Daughter After God's Own Heart
- The Remarkable Women of the Bible
- Small Changes for a Better Life
- Walking with the Women of the Bible
- A Wife After God's Own Heart
- A Woman After God's Own Heart®
- A Woman After God's Own Heart®— Daily Devotional
- A Woman's Daily Walk with God
- A Woman's Guide to Making Right Choices
- A Woman's High Calling
- A Woman's Walk with God
- A Woman Who Reflects the Heart of Jesus
- A Young Woman After God's Own Heart
- A Young Woman After God's Own Heart— A Devotional
- A Young Woman's Guide to Discovering Her Bible
- A Young Woman's Guide to Making Right Choices
- A Young Woman's Guide to Prayer
- A Young Woman Who Reflects the Heart of Jesus

Study Guides

- Beautiful in God's Eyes Growth & Study Guide
- Finding God's Path Through Your Trials Growth & Study Guide
- Following God with All Your Heart Growth & Study Guide
- Life Management for Busy Women Growth & Study Guide
- Loving God with All Your Mind Growth & Study Guide
- Loving God with All Your Mind Interactive Workbook
- A Mom After God's Own Heart Growth & Study Guide
- The Remarkable Women of the Bible Growth & Study Guide
- Small Changes for a Better Life Growth & Study Guide
- A Wife After God's Own Heart Growth & Study Guide
- A Woman After God's Own Heart® Growth & Study Guide
- A Woman Who Reflects the Heart of Jesus Growth & Study Guide

Children's Books

- A Girl After God's Own Heart
- A Girl After God's Own Heart Devotional
- A Girl's Guide to Making Really Good Choices
- A Girl's Guide to Discovering Her Bible
- God's Wisdom for Little Girls
- A Little Girl After God's Own Heart

Books by Jim George

- 10 Minutes to Knowing the Men and Women of the Bible
- The Bare Bones Bible® Handbook
- The Bare Bones Bible® Handbook for Teens
- A Boy After God's Own Heart
- A Boy's Guide to Discovering His Bible
- A Boy's Guide to Making Really Good Choices
- A Dad After God's Own Heart
- A Husband After God's Own Heart
- Know Your Bible from A to Z
- A Leader After God's Own Heart
- A Man After God's Own Heart
- A Man After God's Own Heart Devotional
- The Man Who Makes a Difference
- One-Minute Insights for Men
- A Young Man After God's Own Heart
- A Young Man's Guide to Discovering His Bible
- A Young Man's Guide to Making Right Choices

Books by Jim & Elizabeth George

- A Couple After God's Own Heart
- A Couple After God's Own Heart Interactive Workbook
- God's Wisdom for Little Boys
- A Little Boy After God's Own Heart

About the Author

Elizabeth George is a bestselling author who has more than nine million books in print. She is a popular speaker at Christian women's events. Her passion is to teach the Bible in a way that changes women's lives.

For information about Elizabeth's books, visit her website:

www.ElizabethGeorge.com